IN THE HOLY LAND

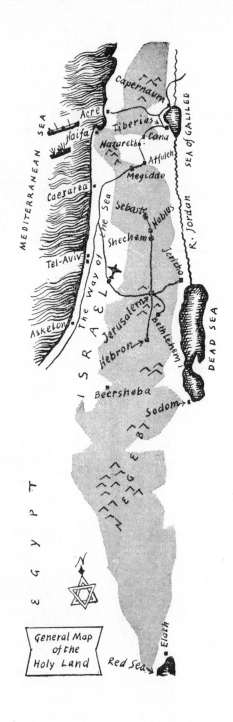

General Map of the Holy Land

IN THE
HOLY LAND

A Journey Along the King's Highways
with
GODFREY C. ROBINSON, B.A., B.D.
and
STEPHEN F. WINWARD, M.A., B.D.

Photographs by the authors and Carol Acworth, and
maps and drawings by L. F. Lupton

WILLIAM B. EERDMANS PUBLISHING COMPANY
GRAND RAPIDS, MICHIGAN

First published 1963

© 1963 Godfrey C. Robinson and Stephen F. Winward

First U.S. edition published by
William B. Eerdmans Publishing Company
July 1968

Reprinted, December 1974

ISBN 0-8028-1169-8

Printed in the United States of America

CONTENTS

ILLUSTRATIONS

INTRODUCTION

I

STEREOSCOPIC PICTURES, which used to be popular in grandfather's day, are again coming into their own. The idea is that by means of two lenses the viewer can enjoy the additional dimension of depth. A stereoscopic picture looks deeper, more solid, more alive.

In this book we invite the reader to join us on a visit to Palestine, viewing the scenes through two lenses, the Bible and the Land. If you see the Holy Land today apart from the Bible, it remains, so to speak, a flat picture. The better way is to see the Book and the Land *together*; and we shall endeavour to do this throughout these chapters.

II

The sub-title, "A Journey Along the King's Highways", was suggested by the message of Moses to the king of Edom. "Now let us pass through your land. We will not pass through field or vineyard, neither will we drink water from a well; we will go along the King's Highway, we will not turn aside to the right hand or to the left, until we have passed through your territory" (Numbers **20**. 17).

There was apparently in ancient Edom a well-defined track for commercial caravans and travellers, of sufficient importance to be associated with the royal name. But within the Holy Land itself we can rightly call all its main roads the King's highways. For in this little country, the land-bridge between Asia and Africa, the servants of the great King passed to and fro on their journeys in His service. What is more, the King Himself, the Lord Jesus Christ, walked along many of these roads.

> *Loving Saviour, Thou didst come*
> *To a lowly Jewish home;*

And didst make for ever Thine
This fair land of Palestine.

In a sense that can never be true of any other land on earth, the roads of Palestine are the King's highways.

III

" The roads across Palestine . . . have determined its history," writes Denis Baly in his book, *The Geography of the Bible.* The force of this statement will become plain as you read on. At the time of writing, the Holy Land is divided, partitioned, though not by agreement, between Jew and Arab. The modern pilgrim cannot always travel the whole length of a road, as was possible formerly when the land was one. He cannot, for example, follow directly in the footsteps of Joseph and Mary from Jerusalem to Bethlehem or of Jesus from Jerusalem to Galilee. The highways are now cut off by the zig-zag, irrational frontiers, and we have been compelled to accept this division in our book.

The historic Way of the Sea described in the three chapters of Part One passes through the territory of the modern state of Israel. Crossing over into the state of Jordan, we shall in the five chapters of Part Two describe the roads within that kingdom radiating outwards from Jerusalem. Finally, because of the unique interest and importance of the Holy City itself, we shall, in the four chapters of Part Three, write of the ways immediately around and within Jerusalem.

IV

Staying at Nazareth, Tiberias, the Mount of Beatitudes, Jerusalem and Bethlehem, we shared together most of the experiences narrated. Occasionally scenes, places or events are described which were experienced by only one of us. But because it would be tiresome to the reader, we have deliberately avoided saying: " A saw this, and B saw that." Most of the experiences were shared, and we have set down our impressions throughout in that way.

The Rev. Leslie Farmer, author of *We Saw the Holy City*, who has lived in the Holy Land, revisited it many times, and is an acknowledged authority on this subject, has been kind enough to read the manuscript, and we are grateful to him for his helpful comments and suggestions. We would also like to acknowledge our indebtedness to the following books and authors for invaluable factual information on the geography, history and archæology of the Holy Land:

> *The Historical Geography of the Holy Land*
> George Adam Smith (Hodder & Stoughton)
> *The Geography of the Bible*
> Denis Baly (Lutterworth Press)
> *Atlas of the Bible*
> L. H. Grollenberg (Nelson)
> *Guide to the Holy Land*
> Eugene Hoad (Franciscan Press)

Except where otherwise stated, all the Scripture quotations are from the American Revised Standard Version of the Bible.

v

It may never be the reader's privilege to visit the Holy Land. But perhaps every day of your life you read the Bible. You will find almost as much of the Bible in this book as there is of present-day Palestine. For this reason also, we hope that the book will be especially useful to day and Sunday School teachers, youth workers, lay preachers, and indeed all those who love and use the Bible. If these chapters help you to see the Holy Land as you read the Holy Scriptures, we shall be well rewarded.

G. C. R.
S. F. W.

PART ONE

The Way of the Sea

CHAPTER ONE

ROUND THE LAKE OF GALILEE

I

THE SUN SHONE from a cloudless sky as we rested for a moment in the burning heat. We had been trudging along the Way of the Sea and were thankful at the eastern end of the Plain of Gennesaret to find a little shack with a cheerful young Jew selling orange-juice.   It carried the sign, " Holy Land Buffet "!

Behind us lay Capernaum with its ruined synagogue hidden by a clump of trees; over to our right rose the Mount of the Beatitudes, the traditional site of the sermon recorded in Matthew's Gospel, chapters 5 to 7.   To our left we could see the blue waters of the Lake of Galilee; and beyond, on the eastern shore, the steep slopes of Gadara.

We opened our Bibles and read again Mark's Gospel, chapter 1.   " Now as He walked by the Sea of Galilee. . . ." So it was along this road, by these very waters, that the Saviour once walked with His disciples.   Somewhere along this shore the fishermen were called from their nets to become fishers of men, and along this road they often walked in conversation with their Master.

In Bible times this Way of the Sea was a main artery, the great highway coming down from Damascus in the north-east, past Mount Hermon, across the territorial boundary marked by the River Jordan, and on through Capernaum, the town where our Lord lived, taught and healed.   After Capernaum, as you can see from the map on p. 13, the road runs alongside the Lake and across the fertile Plain of Gennesaret, behind the huddle of trees that now marks the site of Magdala; and thence turns up into the Galilean hills.   It emerges from these between Nazareth and Mount Tabor, and crosses the great Plain of Esdraelon, the battlefield of the ancient world. Through the historic Pass of Megiddo, it goes on towards the sea, through the maritime Plains of Sharon and Philistia, and so down into Egypt.

This was the historic life-line between the two great civilizations of the Euphrates and the Nile, a link by which the fabled wealth of the eastern deserts reached the Mediterranean Sea and the West.   Along this way came cavalcades of merchants and soldiers, camel trains and armies.   It was trodden by patriarchs and Apostles; parts of it were as familiar to the Lord Jesus as the road along which you travel to work each day. For it went through Capernaum and Bethsaida, and by-passed Nazareth.   And He *walked* along it.   What a strong, vigorous figure the Saviour must have been; the " pale Galilean " is a figment of the poet Swinburne's imagination! This stony track alongside the sea, climbing rugged hills and traversing great plains, was indeed the King's highway.

II

The Way of the Sea begins, as we have said, at Damascus, the largest oasis and one of the oldest cities in the world; the scene of the conversion of the greatest of all Christian thinkers and missionaries, Saul of Tarsus.   After leaving Damascus, the traveller sees away to his right the snow-capped peak of Hermon.   It is at the foot of Mount Hermon, near the site of the ancient city of Dan (which was the northern limit of the Holy Land), that the four streams rise which unite into the one River Jordan north of Lake Huleh.   One of these streams gushes forth impressively from the cavern of a cliff.   The grotto here was dedicated by the Greeks to their god Pan, and near to this shrine Herod the Great built a temple of white marble in honour of the Roman emperor, Augustus.   Philip, who later became tetrarch of the region, enlarged the town, which then became known as Cæsarea.

" Now when Jesus came into the district of Cæsarea Philippi . . . ."   It was to this place that our Lord came with His disciples, and here He was acknowledged by Simon Peter and the rest as the Messiah, the Son of God (Matt. **16**. 13–20).   Six days, or according to the inclusive Jewish reckoning, eight days later, He was transfigured in the presence of Moses and Elijah, and Peter, James and John.   As He was praying, perhaps on one of the lower spurs of this mountain, " the appearance of His countenance was altered, and His raiment became dazzling white "—as the hymn puts it, " Whiter than Hermon's whitest snow " (Luke **9**. 29).   The lovely snow-capped summit of Mount Hermon can often be seen from long distances in the Holy Land.   It was an uplifting sight to the weary labourer or traveller, and became associated in people's minds with the refreshing night-dews (Psalm **133**. 3).

South of Mount Hermon is the Huleh basin, at the southern

end of which is the lake of that name.   This land of swamps and
of the papyrus reed is now being reclaimed by the modern
state of Israel.   Continuing south-westwards below Lake
Huleh, the Way of the Sea crossed the Jordan by the Bridge of
Jacob's Daughters, close by the place where the river enters a
narrow gorge and descends to the Lake of Galilee.   In our
Lord's time this was the boundary between the tetrarchy of
Philip and that of Herod Antipas—just as it is today between
the state of Syria and Israel.   It was probably here, east of the
Jordan and just north of the Lake that the miracle of the Feeding of the Five Thousand took place, close to the town of
Bethsaida Julias.   Although at the time of our visit political
tensions made it impossible for us to land at Bethsaida Julias,
we were able to see the place from a boat.   Here in spring-
time luscious green grass grows in the valleys and plains, and
Peter, who was an eye-witness of the event, remembered how
on that memorable occasion, his Master " commanded them
all to sit down by companies upon the green grass "(Mark
6. 39).

III

For the Christian, the first glimpse of the Lake of Galilee,
associated so closely with the ministry of our Saviour, is a
deeply-moving experience.   We first saw it when travelling
down the road from Nazareth to Tiberias, a road which drops
steeply from the hills of Galilee to the Lake 680 feet below sea-
level.   There deep down below it lies like a glimmering blue
jewel surrounded by green and brown hills.   Perhaps the first
impression on the traveller accustomed from infancy to hearing
Bible stories about the Sea of Galilee, is that of its smallness.
For this is a *lake*, not unlike our own English Windermere or
Derwentwater; or our Scottish Lomond or one of the other
lochs.   Today, however, the hills surrounding the Lake of
Galilee are not wooded.

The Lake, which measures some thirteen miles by seven, is
pear-shaped, being widest and deepest at the northern end.   It
has been called by several different names—Galilee, Tiberias,

Gennesaret, Chinnereth (or Kinnereth)—the last of which, the Hebrew word for " harp ", is suggested by its shape. The surface, reflecting the colour of the sky, appears deep blue. In some places, especially to the east, the hills descend steeply to the water; in others there is an intervening plain. The general scene today is one of softness and tranquillity, almost rustic and idyllic. But it was very different in Christ's day. In the centuries before Turks and Arabs cut down the trees, there was abundant vegetation, and the hills were covered with trees. Then there were as many as eight, and possibly ten, populous cities round the shore—not only Tiberias as now, but also Magdala, Bethsaida, Capernaum, Chorazin, Taricheae, Gadara, Hippos, and Gergesa. Indeed, in those days, the Lake must have been almost surrounded by town or dwellings, and was a scene of bustling activity.

Today one sees an occasional sail or a few motor-boats; in our Lord's day there was a considerable fishing industry, and fishing boats were plentiful. But visitors to the Holy Land will discover that in recent years new Jewish communities have been springing up around Lake Galilee. We visited one such " kibbutz " near the southern tip, where the Jordan leaves the Lake, and were impressed by the orderly, attractive community buildings. In a few decades—who knows?—it may happen that the shores of Galilee will become populous, a hive of industry, once more.

IV

Just about one mile south of Tiberias are the hot springs and baths of el-Hammam. Famed throughout the ancient world for their healing properties, they were visited by invalids from far and wide. They are still a centre of attraction, and as our hotel adjoined these thermal springs we were often able to mingle with the motley crowd of Israeli men and women who had come to visit them. The Israelis today are developing Tiberias as a holiday centre, so that modern tourists are rediscovering the attractions that Herod Antipas found there many centuries ago. To reach our chalets on the hill-side,

B

from which there were lovely views of the whole Lake, we
passed beneath trees from which issued a never-ceasing chorus
of bird song.   At our very first meal we were served with the
musht (the Arabic word for " comb "), or Peters' Perch.   This
fish, caught in the Lake, is noted for the marked pouch under
its mouth, and may well have been the kind of fish in which
Peter found the coin (Matt. **17**. 27).

Tiberias, the only town on the lake-side today, was founded
by Herod Antipas (the Herod of Luke **3**. 1; **9**. 7; and **23**. 8)
somewhere about the year A.D. 18 to 20. Herod made it his
capital.   Named in honour of the gloomy tyrant, the emperor
Tiberius, it must have been an imposing city, with citadel,
palace and forum, and a wall three miles long.   But as it was
built over a cemetery, no true Jew would live there, and its
population would therefore have been half-Greek.   It is
interesting that there is no reference in the Gospels to our Lord
having visited this town; but, by a strange reversal of fortune,
it became the seat of the Sanhedrin in the second century A.D.
Here the important Jewish sacred books, the Mishna and the
Jerusalem Talmud, were written.

Modern Tiberias, with its shops and rather squalid market,
is not particularly attractive, although it may develop rapidly
with the growth of the tourist trade.   As we sat drinking tea on
the quayside, where fishing nets made of nylon were hanging
on the trees alongside, we watched a motor-boat setting out to
fish.   Once again we were made aware of that incongruous
combination of old and new to be seen almost everywhere in
the Holy Land today.

v

The Sea of Tiberias, as John calls it (John **21**. 1), is notor-
iously subject to sudden storms.   Closely shut in by the hills,
the wind can rush down the narrow gorges which open on to
the Lake, whipping the water into fury.   It was during one
such " great storm of wind ", when the waves were beating into
the boat, that the waters heard the voice of the Master and
hushed their raging (Mark **4**. 35–41).   But on the morning

when we set out to cross the Lake from Tiberias to " the other side ", all was calm and peaceful. Very few sailing-boats were to be seen, since the motor-boat has largely replaced them. Normally these go out in " flotillas ", and one can catch the gleam of their tiny lights across the water at night.

We were intrigued to find that our boat was called the *Capernaum*, and it was on board this boat crossing over to Ain Gev that we bought a tin of " Galilee Sardines ". Two main kinds of fish are still caught in the Lake—the *musht*, to which reference has already been made, and a little sardine-like fish about two inches long. These latter may well have been the fishes that the lad was carrying for his lunch on the occasion of the feeding of the multitude (John **6**. 9). Nowadays there is a cannery at Ain Gev on the eastern shore, where our boat put in and stopped for an hour or so. The tins are packed in brightly coloured cartons containing on one side a picture of the mosaic of the loaves and fishes at Tabgha; and on the other, the story of the Feeding of the Five Thousand from the New Testament!

This isolated pocket of Israeli territory on the east of the Lake, almost surrounded by Syria, is called in the Gospels " the country of the Gerasenes " (Mark **5**. 1). Here it was, when Jesus cured the demoniac, that a herd of swine " rushed down the steep bank into the sea, and were drowned in the sea " (Mark **5**. 13). We walked part of the way into the hills to see the rugged slopes of Gadara more clearly, and what was left of some very ancient tombs. Here also at Ain Gev we had the opportunity of photographing a large shoal of fishes. From the shore they could be seen clearly alongside a boat, and we were reminded of the incident recorded in John **21**. 6 that took place after the Resurrection, when the fish were visible to the Lord on the shore, but not to the disciples in the boat.

VI

In returning diagonally north-westwards across Lake Galilee from Ain Gev to Capernaum, we could see clearly away to our right the grassy plain near Bethsaida Julias, where Jesus fed the multitude. It must have been among those hills there in the

background that He retired to pray after the miracle. Mean-
while, the disciples " got into a boat, and started across the sea
to Capernaum. It was now dark and Jesus had not yet come
to them. The sea rose because a strong wind was blowing.
When they had rowed about three or four miles, they saw Jesus
walking on the sea and drawing near to the boat " (John **6**. 17–
19). They were glad to take Him aboard, and soon reached
land. Next morning when the people discovered that the
Teacher had gone " they themselves got into the boats and
went to Capernaum, seeking Jesus " (John **6**. 24). We were
now crossing the same part of the Lake, and as the boat
approached Capernaum, were gazing at the very landscape
that Peter, Andrew, James and John had seen many a morning
as they returned, spent and weary, from a night's fishing. It
was the same scene, yet so different. There stood the same
everlasting hills, strong, serene. But where was the city of
Capernaum, full of life and activity, in which the fishermen disciples had lived? A clump of trees, a little quayside, a Franciscan House, a ruined synagogue, a few old stones—that is all.

But the ruined synagogue which we saw twice, once in the day-
light, and then again by moonlight, was a sacred spot. Some
believe it to be the actual synagogue of our Lord's time, in
which He taught with authority, healed the man with an
unclean spirit and gave His discourse on the Bread of Life
(Mark **1**. 21–28; John **6**. 59). But this is unlikely, since the
Roman general Titus during the Jewish war, and the emperor
Hadrian after the later Jewish Rebellion, destroyed all the
synagogues of the Holy Land. It probably, however, stands on
the same site, follows a similar plan, and may even have
incorporated into it some of the stones of the synagogue of
Christ's time. Even in ruins it is imposing, and on some of the
huge blocks, palms, grapes and various other designs have been
sculptured. Although it was a Jewish synagogue, the architecture is Græco-Roman, and brought to mind the tribute paid
to the builder of the original synagogue, the Roman centurion,
" For he loves our nation, and he built us our synagogue "
(Luke **7**. 5).

From the synagogue the Lord went direct to Peter's house
(Mark **1**. 29). We saw the ancient mosaic that marks the
site of a church built over what was then believed to be the site
of the disciple's dwelling, where Simon's mother-in-law was
healed that sabbath morning. We lingered at the quayside.
It was probably at, or near, this ancient quayside that Matthew
worked as a custom's clerk. Perhaps he helped to collect the
toll on passing merchandise; for the Way of the Sea entered the
territory of Herod Antipas near to Capernaum. What a
contrast between the prosperous city of his day with its streets
and crowds, and the deserted site of today, covered with tall,
tangled weeds! " And you, Capernaum, will you be exalted
to heaven? You shall be brought down to Hades " (Matt. **11**.
23). The Master's prophecy has been fulfilled; Chorazin,
Bethsaida, Capernaum, the cities which rejected His message,
have all gone down to judgment and desolation.

VII

From Capernaum the Way of the Sea continues alongside
the Lake in the direction of the fertile plain of Gennesaret.
This is holy ground indeed; for the Lord must often have
walked this way. We came to El Tabgha, or Seven Springs, a
place with a plentiful supply of water, and rich in vegetation.
This is thought by some to be part of the site of " Bethsaida of
Galilee ", the city of Andrew, Peter and Philip, referred to in
Mark **6**. 45; Luke **10**. 13; John **1**. 44 and **12**. 21. Bethsaida
Julias, where the 5,000 were fed, was almost certainly a
different town situated north-east of the Lake. Some archæologists believe that the latter was the only Bethsaida; others
think that there were two towns of that name in our Lord's
time. It is possible that Capernaum and Bethsaida of Galilee
were so extensive as to form almost one district.

Down by the lake-side is a little church in basalt, built over a
massive rock called the " Mensa Christi ", or Table of Christ.
Here according to ancient tradition the Risen Lord welcomed
His disciples, and prepared breakfast for them (John **21**. 9).
Here, too, may well have been the little bay where the disciples

were first called at their fishing. Nearby are the famous
Tabgha mosaics, discovered in 1932, part of a church built not
later than the fourth century. We spent some time looking at
these lovely mosaics—birds and fishes, and beasts and flowers,
as well as a representation of the loaves and fishes. The
Christians who decorated their church in this way must, like
their Master, have had a real love of nature.

It is near this spot that a road branches off at right-angles to
the shore, and climbs steeply to the Mount of the Beatitudes,
believed to be the place overlooking the Lake where the great
Sermon was preached (Matt. **5.** 1). We stayed at the hospice
on the Mount, enjoying the wonderful views north-eastwards to
Capernaum, south-westwards along the Plain of Gennesaret—
and over the Lake to the mountains of Syria. One evening
before sunset we gathered on the slopes of the hill and read
through the entire " Sermon ", in Matthew's Gospel, chapters
5 to **7**. As our eyes kept straying from the Gospel page to the
surrounding scenery, it was noteworthy how many of the
things mentioned in our Lord's discourse could actually be seen.

The next day we crossed the Plain of Gennesaret, which
gives to the Lake one of its names (Luke **5.** 1). The Plain is
four miles broad, and is exceptionally fertile. This is " the
land of Gennesaret "—where they brought to Jesus " all that
were sick, and besought Him that they might only touch the
fringe of His garment " (Matt. **14.** 34–36). South of the
Plain where the hills close in on the Lake is Magdala, home of
Mary Magdalene. According to the Jewish historian Josephus,
in Gospel times it had 4,000 inhabitants and a fleet of 230
boats! Today it is a tiny village of fisher-folk huddled behind
a few trees. And not far beyond Magdala—further south, is
Tiberias—where we began our account of this journey round
the shores of the Lake.

VIII

The Way of the Sea leaves the Lake of Galilee by the " Wadi
el Hamam, the Valley of Pigeons ", just behind Magdala—a
name, by the way, which means " the Tower ", for probably a

fort once stood here to guard this important road junction. This was the King's highway on His journeyings from Capernaum up to Nazareth. As the road begins to climb into the hills of Galilee, it passes beneath the Horns of Hattin, a mountain which looks like an Arabian saddle. It was here in A.D. 1187 that the Saracen leader Saladin decisively defeated the Crusaders. As George Adam Smith writes in *The Historical Geography of the Holy Land*, " A militant and truculent Christianity, as false as the relics of the ' true Cross ' round which it was rallied, met its judicial end within view of the scenes where Christ proclaimed the Gospel of Peace, and went about doing good."

Along this road we must continue, but first let us take a lingering look back at the Lake, the main scene of our Saviour's ministry, now disappearing from sight. With gratitude we lift up our hearts in thanksgiving to God that the words of Isaiah have been gloriously fulfilled (Isaiah 9. 1, 2); " In the latter time He will make glorious the way of the sea, the land beyond the Jordan, Galilee of the nations. The people who walked in darkness have seen a great light; those who dwelt in a land of deep darkness, on them has light shined."

CHAPTER TWO

NAZARETH

I

" JESUS OF NAZARETH "—to the end of time, the name of Jesus, the Saviour of the world, will be linked with one particular city. To this place, after the death of Herod the Great, Joseph and Mary returned from Egypt with the infant Jesus. Here " the child grew and became strong, filled with wisdom; and the favour of God was upon him " (Luke 2. 40). Here He lived in a cottage home, worked as a carpenter, and went to synagogue on the sabbath, until He was about thirty years of age.

It has been customary to represent the Nazareth in which Jesus lived as an obscure village, cut off from the great events of the day, secluded from the busy world. But was this really the case? The Way of the Sea did not pass directly through Nazareth; but it passed close by, just a little to the east, and the south. The great caravan route between Damascus and the sea divided into two routes on reaching the Lake of Galilee and, as you can see from the map on page 13, the traffic on this great arterial road passed round the foot of the hill on which Nazareth stood. It then continued across Esdraelon to the Pass of Megiddo, and so along the coastal plain to distant Egypt.

Thus the traffic of this great arterial road passed round the foot of the hill on which Nazareth stood. The boy Jesus, by taking a short walk to the edge of the shallow basin in the hills in which Nazareth lay, could have seen the caravans, the merchants, the travellers, the soldiers, the whole pageant of movement along the Way of the Sea. A further short walk, and He could easily have mingled with them. Or, had He walked in the opposite direction towards Sepphoris, He could have overlooked the other mighty highway from Acre running into the interior towards the cities of the Decapolis. From the travellers on these roads, news would reach Him from all over the known world, and here He would meet many of the characters which later were to appear in His parables and stories.

II

It is probably true to say that the highway along which the King walked more than any other, was that which joined Capernaum, the headquarters of His Galilean ministry, with Nazareth, His home town. And now we were travelling this very road, leaving behind the tranquil beauty of the Lake, and ascending steeply into the hills. Capernaum is about twenty-five miles from Nazareth, and for, some distance the road follows the ancient Way of the Sea. But it diverges to pass through Cana of Galilee, and then Nazareth. We remembered

that this was the road up which the royal official climbed to
Cana, in order to beg Jesus to " come down " and heal his son
(John 4. 46-54). Great was his faith to make such a long
journey, and great his request that Jesus should walk over
twenty miles to bring this blessing. Close to Cana there is a
fertile region which since medieval times has been called " the
field of the ears of corn ". This is said to be the place where
Jesus was rebuked by the Pharisees for permitting His disciples
to pluck ears of corn on the sabbath (Mark 2. 23-28).

And so we came to Cana, now a small and somewhat squalid
village, and yet named in almost every Christian marriage
service, from the humblest to those of high society. Here it
was that Jesus performed " the first of His signs " by trans-
forming the water into wine (John 2. 1-11). It must be frankly
admitted that the site of the Cana mentioned four times in
John's Gospel cannot now be established with any certainty.
There are at least three, if not four places of that name. Some
authorities believe that Khirbet Kana, about eight miles due
north of Nazareth, is the Cana of the Bible; others favour
Kefr Kanna, three and a half miles north-east of Nazareth.
In this latter place there are Greek and Latin churches.

We stopped there first to read from our Bibles the familiar
story, and then to enter the Franciscan church built over the
supposed site of the marriage-feast. There certainly was an
ancient church on this spot, built probably in the sixth century.
We saw a little of the floor of this Byzantine church, together
with an old well-mouth and a cistern. Here, too, was a large
flagon-like water pot, found on or near the excavated site. It
was said to be of the same type as those mentioned in the Gospel story; although the Evangelist says that these held from
twenty to thirty gallons each. We remembered, too, that
Cana was the home of Nathanael, who is also called Bartholo-
mew, one of the twelve disciples. A chapel at the northern
end of the village is dedicated to him. But chiefly we wanted
to see the ancient well, just near the village, although at the
time of our visit this was dry. Was it from this same well that
the water was drawn that later " blushed to wine " ? Slowly

we walked back along the road thinking again of the might and majesty of the One Who " at Cana in Galilee " manifested His glory. As later we continued our journey to Nazareth, three and a half miles away, we saw an Arab in long white robes following an old wooden plough drawn by a donkey and an ox, " unequally yoked together " (2 Cor. **6**. 14, A.V.).

III

A well-known hymn refers to " the fair green hills of Galilee, that girdle quiet Nazareth ". " Girdle "—that is correct, for the town is in a saucer or basin, with the hills all round. It is situated on the ranges of Lower Galilee, on the very edge of the Plain of Esdraelon, 1,600 feet above the level of the sea. Nazareth is not mentioned in the Old Testament, nor by the Jewish historian Josephus. But it was evidently of some size and importance, for in the New Testament it is never called a village, but always a city. Although it is now in Israel, the population is still largely Arab. We noticed, however, that new Jewish houses and flats are being built on the perimeter.

Something at this point seemed to have gone wrong with our travel arrangements, and we were told that there were no beds for us in the little hotel where we were having meals. Beds were found for us in a maternity hospital! The French Sisters of St. Vincent de Paul gave us a warm welcome and treated us with great kindness. Then immediately after breakfast, stopping only for a short session with guide-book and map, we sauntered along the street and poked around the shops. In the old town, a deep groove about two feet wide ran down the centre of the street, and along this the donkeys trotted with their riders. The shops were dark recesses, windowless al-coves; but usually a variety of goods were displayed outside in the bright sunshine. There were donkeys and mules, goats and chickens, crockery and pans, furniture and food, insects and smells, urchins and friars, men and women, all in colourful and fascinating confusion. This was the morning " rush hour "; but nobody seemed to be in a hurry. There was an air of leisure, with groups of men sitting round sipping thick, black, mud-like coffee.

Some of the men in our party fancied themselves as Arabs, and bought themselves *kafiyehs*—as the white flowing head-cloth with its black rope ring is called. Or was it to seek protection from the fierce heat of the sun? It was in the streets of Nazareth, in so many ways like these same streets to-day, that Jesus had walked. In the market-place He had watched the children playing at weddings and funerals—or sometimes sulkily refusing to play anything (Matt. **11**. 16–17). Perhaps in its bazaar He had once seen " a merchant in search of fine pearls " (Matt. **13**. 45).

IV

But where exactly had the house stood in which He had lived at Nazareth, with Joseph and Mary, with His brothers James, Joses, Judas and Simon, and with His sisters? We are not told anything directly about that home in the Gospels. But are not the sayings, parables and stories of Jesus like windows, through which we can peep into it? It is small; one lamp placed on a stand gives light to all who are in the house. Mother is busy making bread, or patching old garments, but not with new cloth; or maybe sweeping the floor carefully in search of a lost coin. Father is giving little loaves or eggs to the hungry children who are asking for food. How wonderful it would be to stand—or better, kneel—on the exact spot, where for so long " the Word . . . dwelt among us " (John **1**. 14). But the place can no longer be known with certainty.

At either end of the large Franciscan Convent are the traditional sacred sites. One of these is known as the Grotto of the Annunciation, where the angel Gabriel is said to have made the announcement to the Virgin Mary that she would be the destined mother of the Messiah. A church built over this cave in 1730 has been removed, and a new Church of the Annunciation was, at the time of our visit, being built. The excavations for this work have disclosed remains of a yet earlier church built by the Crusaders (destroyed in 1263), and of an ancient Byzantine building. At the other end of the Franciscan Convent beneath the Church of St. Joseph (built in 1914), is the traditional site of the house of Joseph and Mary. There is a crypt beneath this church, where can be seen a small area of mosaic pavement of the original Byzantine structure. Descending again beneath this, we entered a cave or grotto.

Did Jesus live on this very spot? Did His mother store things in these " cupboard spaces " in the wall and the ground? Was it here that He helped His father make yokes, and tables and stools? We do not really know. But we do know two things. These sites were clearly regarded as sacred when the ancient Byzantine churches were built. Secondly, the grotto is not impossible as a dwelling place. As the guide-book truly says, " It is not difficult to find in Palestine, and especially in Nazareth, small houses attached to the side of a hill, which houses are composed in the upper storey of stone work, and in the lower of a grotto hollowed out of the natural rock. Such was the appointment of the humble dwelling of Mary." Perhaps this humble dwelling place *was* the scene of those hidden years.

v

We walked right through the town, and came to the Virgin's Fountain, or Mary's Well. The spring is surrounded by a wall, built during the Turkish occupation. An Arab guide on the spot led us a little further back, to the Orthodox Church of St. Gabriel, which was dark and gloomy. Here, he explained to us, the spring bubbles out of the hill-side; and lifting up a paving stone of the church we listened to the flowing water, which is led by a conduit pipe to the Virgin's Fountain, some yards further down the road. Looking through an iron grating we saw also the disused steps leading down to the original well. Springs change little during the centuries and it must have been here, or very close at hand, that Mary came to draw water, no doubt often accompanied by her Son.

From the roof of the Church, there is a fine view of Nazareth and the surrounding hills, and we took special note of a large

and conspicuous building high on the hill-side. We decided
to walk up to it. But shortage of time and the heat of the sun
made us change our minds about how to get there. And so
in an old taxi we were jogged and bumped along a steep, stony
track, up to the Church of Jesus-Adolescent. We were well
rewarded with a magnificent view of the hills round Nazareth,
including the rounded dome of Tabor about five miles distant,
and the remoter mountains of Gilboa. On these hill-sides
the boy Jesus must often have romped and played, like the
laughing jolly boys who now crowded round us, intensely
interested in our cameras. In the church there is a lovely
statue of Jesus-Adolescent. The sculptor, in a quite remarkable way, has embodied in the stone something of the simplicity,
integrity and consecration of the Boy Who increased daily in
the favour of God.

Not that Jesus spent most of His time playing on the hills
around His home. There was work to be done! We do not
know how old He was when Joseph died. But from that time,
as the eldest son, He would be fully responsible for the main-
tenance of a family, which numbered at least eight, and
possibly more (the number of His sisters is not stated in the
Gospel story). " The carpenter's son " was no doubt
Himself a carpenter—although in those days a joiner not only
worked with wood, but also helped to build houses. Perhaps
the workshop was beneath the house, like, if not identical with,
" the workshop of Joseph " now to be seen beneath the church
of that name. Later the great Teacher drew some of His
illustrations from that workshop—the irritating speck of saw-
dust in the eye, the plank leaning against the wall, the house
well built to withstand the storm, the yoke well-fitting which
made the burden light (Matt. 7. 3; 7. 25; 11. 30). Down in
the streets of Nazareth we saw a carpenter amid his ploughs
and yokes, about to set off on a donkey. To meet a real carpenter in Nazareth makes one realize what a down-to-earth,
flesh and blood affair, the Gospel is. *Verbum caro hic factum est*,
says the inscription beneath a painting in the Annunciation
Grotto—" Here the Word was made flesh ".

VI

Jesus not only played and toiled; He also worshipped. At Nazareth, Luke tells us, " He went to the synagogue, as His custom was, on the sabbath day " (Luke 4. 16). Nothing now remains of that synagogue, but the Greek Catholic Church, in the middle of the old town, is said to be built on the site. We made our way there on more than one occasion, up the narrow overarched street, thronged with animals and men. Inside the domed church, which was brightly painted with a rich variety of colours, the altar was separated from the nave, not by a solid *ikonostasis*, but by a veil—recalling the inspired comment of a reformed theologian on Greek Orthodox worship, " So the veil of the temple has been stitched together again! " Outside this Church, to the left of the forecourt, there is a small hall, said to be on the site of the ancient synagogue. It could be that part of the floor dates back to our Lord's time.

Luke describes how the Saviour re-visited this synagogue, probably soon after the beginning of His ministry in Galilee. Already well known as Teacher, Healer and Prophet, He was invited to " read the second lesson ". He selected a passage from the Book of Isaiah and read, " The Spirit of the Lord is upon me, because He has anointed me to preach good news to the poor. He has sent me to proclaim release to the captives and recovering of sight to the blind, to set at liberty those who are oppressed, to proclaim the acceptable year of the Lord " (Luke 4. 18, 19).

After taking the speaker's chair on the platform, He addressed His own townsfolk. At first they were impressed by the gracious words of His lips, but later this admiration turned to cynicism as they recalled that He was only an ordinary person, " just one of us ". He proceeded to remind them that a prophet is never honoured in his own country. Was it not a widow of *Phœnicia* who gave hospitality to the prophet Elijah; and Naaman the *Syrian* who came for healing to the prophet Elisha? These appreciative references to Gentiles were deeply offensive to the narrow nationalism of His Jewish hearers. In fury they rose up, threw Him out of the synagogue, and hustled Him along to the brow of the hill on which the town was built. This hill has for long been identified with a conspicuous headland, the Mount of Precipitation, overlooking the Plain of Esdraelon.

We made our way there one morning, amid a profusion of wild flowers, passing the Chapel of the Fright, a place from which His mother is said to have watched the event in agony and dismay. It is not clear from the Gospel exactly what happened. When they reached the hill-top to cast Him down headlong, He passed through the midst of them and went away. Perhaps, as with the soldiers later in Gethsemane, they were overawed by the serenity and majesty of His bearing and personality. None-the-less it was a stark tragedy—the rejection at Nazareth. What a paradox! The people who knew Him best of all, knew Him not at all. Here in the town where Jesus spent so many years the people could have said in a unique sense, " The Word was made flesh and *dwelt among us*." But did they behold His glory, full of grace and truth? Alas, no. Their hasty verdict was " Is not this the carpenter's son? "

CHAPTER THREE

THE PLAINS OF ESDRAELON AND SHARON

I

IT WAS TIME to leave Nazareth. We wanted to see so many other places that from our Bibles we seemed to have known from early childhood. We wanted to continue over these hills and across these plains, following the King's highways. So our journey took us through the Plains of Esdraelon and Sharon.

As we said in Chapter One, the Way of the Sea linked the ancient civilizations of the Euphrates and the Nile. All the

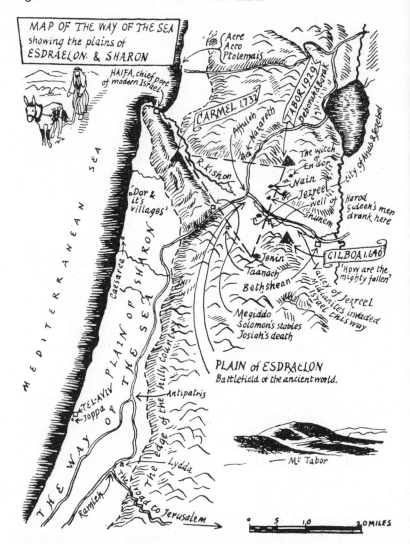

MAP OF THE WAY OF THE SEA
showing the plains of
ESDRAELON & SHARON

HAIFA, chief port
of modern Israel

Acre
Acco
Ptolemais

CARMEL 1,732

TABOR 1929

Deborah & Barak

Affuleh

Mt. Nazareth

R. Kishon

The Witch
of Endor

city of Anab & Jezebel

Nain

Jezreel

well of

Shunem

Harod
Gideon's men
drank here

'Dor &
it's
villages'

Caesarea

PLAIN OF SHARON

GILBOA 1,640
'How are the
mighty fallen'

Jenin

Taanach

Beth shean

Valley of Jezreel
Midianites invaded
Israel this way

Megiddo
Solomon's stables
Josiah's death

PLAIN of ESDRAELON
Battlefield of the ancient world.

MEDITERRANEAN SEA

THE WAY OF THE SEA

TEL AVIV
Joppa

Antipatris

The edge of the Hilly Country

— Mt Tabor

Lydda

The Road to Jerusalem

Ramleh

0 5 10 20 MILES

way there were changes of scenery—river valley, mountain
range, desert, city and oasis, plateau, lake-side, narrow pass,
coastal plain. But no part of this long journey could have been
more pleasant to the traveller than the route across the great
Plain of Esdraelon. This rich and beautiful plain was, however, stained with the blood of armies; it was the battlefield

By the Lake of Galilee

Synagogue at Capernaum

3. *From the Mount of the Beatitudes looking across the Lake to Gadara*

4. *Plain of Gennesaret*

General view of Nazareth

Arab Mother and Children

7. *Plain of Esdraelon*

8. *Entrance to the Pass of Megiddo*

of the ancient world. This was the cockpit of the human race, the arena in which Hebrew and Canaanite, Midianite and Syrian, Egyptian and Assyrian, Babylonian and Greek, Seleucid and Ptolemy, Roman and Arab, Crusader and Turk, have all fought, and sustained defeat or won victory. Small wonder that the Plain of Esdraelon, or Megiddo, has given its name to the predicted last great struggle between the nations— the battle of Armageddon (Rev. **16**. 16).

Look closely at the map of the Plain of Esdraelon on page 32. As you can see, the plain is in the shape of a triangle. As we said farewell to Nazareth we planned first of all to visit the places of Biblical interest on the eastern side—Tabor, Endor, Nain, Shunem and Jezreel.

II

Jesus must have seen Tabor more frequently than any other mountain. As He climbed the hills round Nazareth, and indeed in the course of many of His journeys in Galilee, its rounded dome would be visible to Him. We made our way out of Nazareth, descending over 1,000 feet to the plain, and then turned eastwards towards Tabor, about five miles away. The contour of the mountain is striking and unmistakable, like the arch of a rainbow. It rises in isolation 1,400 feet above the plain, and almost 1,900 feet above sea level. Jeremiah says that Nebuchadnezzar, conspicuous as compared with other rulers, was " like Tabor among the mountains " (Jer. **46**. 18). To the Psalmist, its strength and beauty was a testimony to the Creator, " Tabor and Hermon joyously praise Thy name " (Psalm **89**. 12).

We started the ascent from Deburieh, a name reminiscent of Deborah, the prophetess in the Book of Judges. In her day the Canaanites occupied the great plain and the approaches to the hills on all sides, thus dividing the Hebrew tribes to the north and south of it. Inspired and led by Deborah, the Hebrew commander Barak assembled his army on the steep slopes of Tabor, out of reach of the iron chariots of the enemy. From this vantage point, Barak could see the chariots of Sisera,

c

the enemy commander, coming through the narrow gap of the
Kishon in the north-west and passing out into the plain, with
Taanach and Megiddo in the background.   As Barak charged
down upon them, a storm broke, turning the plain into a
quagmire.   The chariots of the enemy were unable to
manœuvre, the horses reared and plunged in panic, and the
swollen River Kishon swept many away.   This decisive victory, so important for the future unity of Israel, is celebrated
in an ancient poem of beauty and vigour—the Song of
Deborah in Judges, chapter 5.

After leaving Deburieh, a steep climb negotiating many
hair-pin bends took us to the summit, which is like a wide platform.   The drivers who had tried to speed with the relentless
zeal of a Jehu (2 Kings 9. 20), opened up the bonnets of their
cars so that the engines could cool down.   In front of us stood
the Franciscan Church of the Transfiguration.   Inside over
the altar there was a large and lovely mosaic of Christ transfigured in glory, conversing with Moses and Elijah, in company with Peter, James and John (Luke 9. 28, 30).   The
remains of earlier Crusader and Byzantine churches, built on
this site, were visible.   Outside, one of the brethren, a modern
St. Francis, was feeding the birds, some of which boldly perched
on his shoulders and head.   Cyril of Jerusalem, Jerome and
others of the fourth century A.D., refer to the tradition that
the Transfiguration of Christ took place on the summit of
Tabor, and this was the generally accepted view from the
fourth to the nineteenth century.   Indeed, the Greek Church
refers to the annual commemoration of the Transfiguration
as " The Feast of Tabor ".

But this time-honoured tradition is no longer held by many.
Not only do the Gospels imply that the Mount of the Transfiguration was near Cæsarea Phillipi (i.e. in the Hermon
range), but it is now also known that the summit of Tabor was
" a built-up area " in our Lord's time, and as such would
hardly have been a suitable place for a quiet retreat.   Nor is
there any certain evidence for the view, inscribed on one of
the walls here, that Tabor was the mountain in Galilee where

Jesus met with His disciples and " more than 500 brethren "
after His resurrection (Matt. **28.** 16 and I Cor. **15.** 6).

III

But we must go back in order to rejoin the main road southwards from Nazareth.   There over to our left, on the northern
slope of Jebel ed-Duhy, or Little Hermon, is the tiny, isolated
village of Nain.   Today it is a cluster of unimpressive houses,
but it was here that our Lord raised the widow's son from the
dead (Luke **7.** 11).   It is interesting to find that there is still a
cemetery just outside the village.   On these same northern
slopes, two miles to the east of Nain, is the little volcanic Tell
Ajoul, the site of Biblical Endor.   Here it was that the dis-
tracted Saul sought out the witch before the battle of Gilboa
(1 Sam. **28.** 7).   Endor and Nain, geographically so close,
spiritually so far apart; in the one a witch trafficked with
death, in the other the Saviour brought back life.

Endor lies east of Nain, but continuing south past the
latter, Shunem can be seen, spread out on the top of a hill just
below Little Hermon.   It looks out southwards across the
Valley of Jezreel to Mount Gilboa.   It was here at Shunem
that " a wealthy woman lived " and frequently entertained
the prophet Elisha in " a small roof chamber with walls "
(2 Kings **4.** 8, 10).   You can read in 2 Kings, chapter **4,** the
fascinating story of her donkey-ride, right across the Plain of
Esdraelon, to see Elisha on Mount Carmel.   And it was as a
result of this journey that her son—like the son of the widow
at Nain, only a few miles away—was raised from the dead.

Just south of Shunem, the fertile Valley of Jezreel runs eastwards, down to Beth-shean and the River Jordan.   This
valley is the main passage from the lands east of Jordan to the
great Plain of Esdraelon.   " In the days when the judges
ruled ", the nomadic Midianites from across the river came
up this way, to plunder the rich plain (Judges **6.** 1–3).   They
camped on the hill-side round Shunem, while Gideon assembled
his men on the other side of the valley, under rugged Mount
Gilboa.   Just below Gideon's army " the spring of Harod "

issued from the hill-side as a broad stream (Judges **7**. 1).
Flanked by reeds and shrubs, it could have been used by the
Midianites as a place of ambush. Perhaps that is why
Gideon selected as soldiers for his campaign only those who
kept alert and watchful even while drinking at the stream; and
with these 300 tested men the hosts of Midian were put to
flight.

Later in Hebrew history, when the Philistines invaded the
great plain, they too encamped on the hill-side at Shunem
(1 Sam. **28**. 4), and from this position advanced to attack Saul
and his army on Mount Gilboa. It was in this battle that
Saul and his sons were slain, and the Hebrews decisively
defeated—the event commemorated in David's beautiful
elegy, "How are the mighty fallen" (1 Sam., chapter **31**,
and 2 Sam. **1**. 17–27). The mutilated body of Saul was later
exposed on the wall of Beth-shean, the strong fortress town
which guards the passage of the Jordan, at the eastern end
of the Valley of Jezreel (1 Sam. **31**. 10). At the other, western,
end of this same valley stood the famous city of Jezreel, a little
north-west of Mount Gilboa. Today a tiny unpretentious
village occupies the site. This was the city of king Ahab and
his wicked queen, Jezebel; here it was that Elijah rebuked
Ahab for the murder of Naboth who "had a vineyard in
Jezreel beside the palace" (1 Kings, chapter **21**). Here, too,
as recorded in 2 Kings **9**. 33, the infamous Jezebel died.

IV

Jezreel stands almost opposite Megiddo, which is at the
other, or more westerly, side of the great plain. As we
travelled across the plain itself, recalling the cavalcade of
Bible heroes and the historic events that took place here, we
passed through the town of Affuleh, and were impressed by
the *modern* Jewish settlements, carefully planned, which are
springing up on all sides. The hard-working pioneers of
modern Israel, and their successors, are helping to restore the
ancient fertility of Esdraelon—although this restoration was
begun long before the establishment of the modern state of

Israel. Rich black-red soil, patches of gold and green, and long avenues of newly planted trees, make a pleasing picture. Here today are vineyards and orchards, wheat and barley, fields of alfalfa and clover, orange and banana groves, and occasional rows of tall, dark, tapering trees. Ancient and modern are found side by side. We saw an Arab following a wooden plough drawn by two donkeys. A hundred yards down the road on the other side, a young Jew in jeans was driving a tractor.

Through such scenes we made our way across the plain to the famous Pass of Megiddo. This is where the Way of the Sea leaves the Plain of Esdraelon, and passing through a fairly long and narrow defile, drops down into the Plain of Sharon by the coast. Through this historic pass many famous and infamous commanders have led their armies, from the Egyptian Pharaoh Thutmose III in the year 1468 B.C. to Viscount Allenby of Megiddo at the head of the allied armies in 1918. In this narrow defile good king Josiah was killed, while rashly attempting to prevent Pharaoh Necho of Egypt from marching to Carchemish on the Euphrates. " And his servants carried him dead in a chariot from Megiddo, and brought him to Jerusalem, and buried him in his own tomb " (2 Kings **23**. 30).

We were glad to be able to visit the site of the ancient city of Megiddo, which stood at the head of this pass. Large-scale excavations have been carried out, and are continuing. Megiddo was already an ancient city when King Solomon rebuilt and fortified it, financing its construction with a special levy (1 Kings **9**. 15). It became one of his " cities of chariots "; and the remains of stables for 110 horses have been excavated. The view from the summit of the mound right across the Plain of Esdraelon is magnificent. We saw it in the fading light of evening, peopled in our thoughts with the pride, pomp and pageantry of empires long ago.

v

Skirting the hills and the lofty Carmel range, the modern highways run north-west from Megiddo, along the valley of

the Kishon to Haifa. This city, with its docks and underground railway, modern shops and blocks of flats, is the chief
port of present-day Israel. A spur of Carmel jutting out towards the deep blue Mediterranean Sea lies just behind the
town. We ascended this, and visited Elijah's Cave—now a
grotto under the altar of a church, said to have been a place
of worship for three thousand years. On this Carmel range,
which at one point towers 1,650 feet above the Kishon Valley,
Elijah faced the prophets of Baal. And it was here that the
Hebrews who had for long been " limping with two different
opinions ", became convinced that the Lord is the true and
living God (1 Kings, chapter 18).

Between Haifa and the Ladder of Tyre, further north
along the coast, in the territory assigned of old to the tribe of
Asher, is the ancient city of Acre. Acre, first mentioned in
Scripture under the name of Acco (Judges 1. 31), later became
the Ptolemais of the New Testament, where the Apostle Paul
on his way to Jerusalem " greeted the brethren and stayed
with them for one day " (Acts 21. 7). Stretching away to the
north of Acre is " the region of Tyre and Sidon " where Jesus
in the course of His journeyings healed the daughter of the
Syrophœnician woman (Mark 7. 24–30). We strolled by the
strong, massive Crusader fortifications of Acre flanking the
sea, and entered the maze of narrow dark alleys in the old
Moslem quarter of the town.

Then, leaving Haifa by the coast road and travelling southwards through the territory known in the Bible as " Dor and
its villages " (Joshua 17. 11), a journey of twenty-five miles
brought us to Cæsarea. Rebuilt by Herod the Great in the
year 10 B.C., this was the political capital and chief port of
Palestine in our Lord's day. Josephus describes how Herod
constructed an artificial harbour, in which great ships could lie
safely at anchor. Massive stones were lowered into the sea
to form a semi-circular jetty 200 feet wide. The remains of
this are now beneath the sea. But the dark outline has in
recent years been observed from the air, and has been inspected
by divers. Here the Roman galleys sailed in with merchants,

soldiers, and governors such as Pontius Pilate, Felix and Festus. From this quayside the Apostle Paul was taken—an ambassador in bonds—to Rome (Acts **27**. 1, 2). Herod beautified the city with palaces and an amphitheatre, with arches and a temple. The site is now covered with sand and weeds, but the work of excavation is going forward.

Ruins of many different ages confront the bewildered visitor. There is the slender minaret of a mosque of the Turkish period, and crumbling arches erected by the Arabs. Massive walls and a moat are the work of the Crusaders, who also built a jetty making use of old Roman pillars. Excavated houses and palaces, statues and pottery of the Roman period took us back in imagination to the days of the Apostles. At Cæsarea, Pontius Pilate had his residence; a stone bearing his name was discovered here in 1961. Here Philip the deacon lived, and Peter preached to Cornelius, who became the first Gentile convert (Acts **21**. 8; **10**. 1, 24). Here Paul was imprisoned for two years; beggarly " guides " even offered to show us " Paul's prison "! Here Paul testified to the Risen Christ before Festus the governor, King Agrippa and all the notables (Acts, chapters **23** to **26**). The Gospel of Luke was probably written at Cæsarea. What a story lies buried beneath the tangled weeds and the drifting sand!

VI

The headland of Carmel is only two hundred yards from the sea, but southwards the maritime plain gradually widens, until at length there are thirty miles between the Mediterranean and the mountains of Judea. Between Carmel and Joppa, it is called the Plain of Sharon; in Biblical times this was covered with forest. Isaiah refers to " the majesty of Carmel and Sharon "—its luxurious vegetation and riches (Is. **35**. 2). The rose, or crocus, of Sharon was famed for its beauty (Song of Solomon **2**. 1). Passing through Sharon, we enjoyed the colour and fragrance of the golden orange groves, in one of which we stopped for our picnic lunch.

At the southern extremity of the plain, on the coast, a mile south of the large modern Jewish town of Tel Aviv, is Jaffa, the Joppa of the Bible. It was at Joppa that Peter raised Tabitha to life, and had his remarkable vision on the roof of the house of Simon the tanner, by the sea (Acts **9**. 36 and **10**. 5, 6). Joppa, too, is associated with the story of Jonah (**1**. 3). Our journey continued south to Lydda, or Lod, and in what remains of the cathedral, we were shown the tomb of St. George. A Christian soldier of high birth, St. George was martyred under Diocletian, a Roman emperor of the early fourth century, and buried at Lydda. It was the Crusader King Richard in the twelfth century who identified him with Merry England, and under Edward III, he became the patron saint of our land. Passing south through Ramleh, we turned eastwards and began to ascend the Judean hills. The road passes the site of Beth-shemesh, and the large village of Kiriath-Jearim—both places associated with the Philistines and the Ark of God (1 Samuel, chapter **6**).

Now with mounting excitement we were making our way upwards, through forests of conifer and cypress, past many a stone cairn and pumping station, along a road which often fell away in precipitous sides, to the goal of every pilgrim's journey—the city of Jerusalem. From these rugged Judean hills, the Jews could look down upon the distant maritime plain, along which passed the Way of the Sea. This we had left at Lydda. Our destination was Jerusalem—but let us take a final look at the great highway between two continents.

Leaving the Plain of Esdraelon by the main exit, the Pass of Megiddo, it entered the Plain of Sharon. Clinging closely to the foothills of Samaria, it passed through Antipatris (Acts **23**. 31) on to Lydda. Then it began to swing westwards from the hills towards the sea. Passing through the cities of Philistia, Ekron, Ashdod and Gaza (1 Sam. **6**. 17), it went across the desert to Egypt. "We now see why the Maritime Plain was so famous a war-path," writes G. A. Smith in *The Historical Geography of the Holy Land*. "It is really not the whole of Palestine which deserves the name of 'The Bridge between Asia and Africa'; it is this level and open coastland along which the embassies and armies of the two continents passed to and fro, not troubling themselves, unless they were provoked, with the barren and awkward highlands to the east." Such then is the ancient and strategic highway, the " Via Maris ", the Way of the Sea, from Hermon to Lydda, that has occupied our first three chapters. We have reached Jerusalem, which we shall now regard as the hub, from which the highways radiate like spokes of a wheel. We turn therefore to the Ways from Jerusalem.

PART TWO

WAYS FROM JERUSALEM

Dothan
NABLUS
Ebal
Shechem
Sychar
Jacob's Well

Sebaste
Samaria

MEDITERRANEAN SEA

Golden Calf

Gerizim

THE WAY TO SAMARIA

Dead Sea scroll and jar

Wadi ferah

Adam?
Damiyeh ford

Valley of Lebonah

Shiloh

THE WAY TO SYCHAR

Bethel

Ai

Beeroth

Khirbat el Mafqar
th'Caliph's Palace

Ramallah

Mizpah

Mt. of Olives
Apostles Fountain
Inn of Good Samaritan

Jebel Quarantal
Mt. of Templation

Kalandia

JERICHO

THE WAY TO BETHLEHEM

Gibeon

Gibeah

JERUSALEM

thus it becometh us...

THE WAY TO JERICHO

Bethany

Rachel's Tomb
Pools of Solomon

THE WAY TO HEBRON

Beit sahur
Village of the Shepherds

Dead Sea scrolls

Shepherds Fields

Bethlehem

Tekoa

Eshcol

Oak of Mamre

HEBRON
Cave of Machpelah
City of Arba

to Beersheba

WILDERNESS OF JESHIMON

DEAD SEA
46 miles long
9 miles wide
1000 ft. deep
1274 ft below sea l.
Lowest point in the
earth's surface
Water 25% solid.

Mosque at Hebron

Ways from Jerusalem

CHAPTER FOUR

THE WAY TO BETHLEHEM

I

THE WAY TO Bethlehem—a dusty, stony track winding over the hills. Joseph leading a donkey, wise men in their colourful robes mounted on camels, the brilliant light of a guiding star. These were the traditional associations. Imagine our surprise therefore when a car drew into the side of the road, and we heard a voice say, " Would you like a ride to Bethlehem? " We had been for a late evening walk along the Kidron Road past the Garden of Gethsemane. But here was a driver going to Bethlehem. The other occupants of the car, he said, would make room for us. We climbed in.

The road we travelled that night was the new one built by the Jordan Government in 1952, because the older and much shorter route passes through Israel territory. This new road winds and swerves for nine tortuous miles, but seemed to us much longer as we climbed in and out of valleys, passing groups of shadowy houses. But there, from the village of Sur Bahir, we caught our first glimpse of the twinkling lights of Bethlehem. So those were the skies where the herald angels sang. Somewhere over there the shepherds kept watch over their flocks. We had known this place all our lives.

II

When Joseph and Mary went up " to the city of David which is called Bethlehem " they would have gone by the more direct route over the Judean hills, a journey of little more than five miles. They would then have seen Herod's palace to the west of Jerusalem, some of the huge stones of

43

which remain today; since the Romans preserved this citadel when they sacked Jerusalem. A mile from the city they would pass the head of the Valley of Rephaim, where the Philistines came up to attack the city in the time of David (2 Sam. 5. 17–25). In earlier days this valley was the boundary between the tribes of Judah and Benjamin (Josh. 15. 8). A further two miles beyond this, Joseph and Mary would have reached what is now called the Well of the Star, because of a tradition that here the Wise Men who had temporarily lost sight of their guiding star paused to drink, and found it again reflected in the water. Further along the road, Holman Hunt, the artist whose name we always associate with the picture of Christ called *The Light of the World*, painted some of his masterpieces. Here his wife Edith later erected in his memory a stone seat commanding a panoramic view eastwards towards the Dead Sea and the mountains of Moab.

Nearer to Bethlehem, where the old and new roads come together, there is a little white dome by the side of the road, the traditional tomb of Rachel the wife of Jacob. " So Rachel died, and she was buried on the way to Ephrath (that is, Bethlehem), and Jacob set up a pillar upon her grave; it is the pillar of Rachel's tomb, which is there to this day " (Gen. 35. 19, 20). " She sank, as did all the ancient saints, on the way to the birthplace of hope," was the comment of one great preacher. It is in connection with the love story of Jacob and his favourite wife, Rachel, " beautiful and lovely " (Gen. 29. 17), and her death in giving birth to Benjamin, the youngest of the sons of Israel, that we first find Bethlehem mentioned in the Bible. When, later on, King Herod slaughtered the infants in the hope of wiping out the newborn " King of the Jews ", the evangelist in poetic vision hears " Rachel weeping for her children " and refusing " to be consoled, because they were no more " (Matt. 2. 18). Today the swift and noisy car as well as the slow and silent-footed camel passes the tomb of Rachel. Garages and petrol stations have invaded peaceful Bethlehem, spreading their

oily trail along this section of the ancient highway. The
traveller reaching the fork where the road to the right continues to Hebron, is glad to turn left and hurry past a pit-like
valley with cultivated terraces, into Bethlehem itself.

III

Along this highway faith and devotion can discern the
footprints of patriarchs, prophets and kings. Here Abraham
drove his flocks and herds towards Hebron (Gen. **13.** 18). It
was to Bethlehem that Ruth the Moabitess came, to seek
refuge beneath the wings of the God of Israel (Ruth **2.** 12).
In the gate of this ancient city Boaz conferred with the elders
and took Ruth to be his wife. In these streets David played
as a boy, and at " the high place " outside the walls was
secretly anointed by Samuel as king in succession to Saul.
Southwards along the Bethlehem road Samuel drove the
heifer to be used in sacrifice at the anointing (1 Sam. **16.** 1–13).
Northwards along this same road David, laden with loaves
and cheeses for his warrior brothers, trudged towards the Vale
of Elah where he was to do battle with the giant Goliath
(1 Sam. **17.** 20). Somewhere in these fields he tended his
sheep, and thoughts were awakened later to be expressed in
the Psalm, " The Lord is my Shepherd . . . He makes me to
lie down in green pastures. He leads me beside still waters "
(Psalm **23.** 1, 2).

Royal Rehoboam passed down this road in his chariot to
supervise the building of his southern fortresses (2 Chron.
11. 5, 6), and Amos of Tekoa " a herdsman, and a dresser of
sycamore trees " (Amos **7.** 14) walked northwards to rebuke
the luxury and vice of the Northern Kingdom. With the lingering memories of David's magnificent reign, " the city of David "
became a symbol of the greater hope of the nation. " But you,
O Bethlehem Ephrathah, who are little to be among the clans
of Judah, from you shall come forth for Me One Who is to be
ruler in Israel, Whose origin is from old, from ancient days "
(Micah **5.** 2). And Micah's prophecy was fulfilled in the
birth of " great David's greater Son ";

Earth has many a noble city;
Bethlehem, thou dost all excel;
Out of thee the Lord from heaven
Came to rule His Israel.

IV

But how does this city, which lives in the imagination of every devoted Christian, appear to the eye of the visitor today? It is small, but intensely interesting. The centre of the town is the large open area, Manger Square, which at certain seasons of the year tends to become one great car park. To the south-east stands the Church of the Nativity and a variety of ecclesiastical buildings; while in the other direction we notice the large modern police barracks and the single main street running along the brow of the hill towards the market-place. A large tree near the police station leans over at a sharp angle, and here in the early morning squats the letter-writer. Illiterate peasants dictate to him their letters; the crowd stands round and listens with interest. Here the private is public. On the further side of the square, in the shade of a few shops and houses, young men in western clothes are sitting on small stools idly playing backgammon. As in most eastern towns, there are always people just sitting and gazing. Perhaps they do it too much—and we in the west too little.

The main street, about half-a-mile in length, occupied by shops and workshops which are little more than alcoves open to the public gaze, leads rather steeply upwards out of one of the corners of the square. Close by this corner stands the mosque with its tall minaret, and here the call to prayer goes forth at the appointed hours. One of these was a great while before sunrise! The muezzin no longer ascends his tower, but calls through an amplifier—in a voice calculated to wake the heaviest sleeper. Owing to the flood of refugees, Moslems are no longer a minority in Bethlehem. But, as far as we could see, nobody seemed to take any notice of these prayer calls.

We sauntered along the main street, taking our time to watch the craftsmen at work, the heavily-burdened donkeys, and occasionally women wearing the tall pointed head-dress reminiscent of fairy stories and dating back to the Crusaders. We climbed the stone steps, and found ourselves in the crowded market—busy, noisy, colourful. It was market day, and we jostled among the traders and their wares. Squalor and poverty were in evidence—but so also was colour and intense human interest.

Were the crowds something like this on that first Christmas Eve? If so, the end of the journey must have been a trying ordeal for Mary. Yet today there is in general a genial, sunny atmosphere about Bethlehem. The students stop and chat on their way home from school, the shopkeepers invite you in for a cup of coffee, the police in their khaki uniforms stop to exchange a greeting. You feel at home in Bethlehem. Somehow you seem to *belong* there.

V

Where exactly in the ancient city was the Lord Jesus born of Mary? Both Matthew and Luke tell us that He was born in Bethlehem, and the latter adds that Mary " laid Him in a manger, because there was no place for them in the inn " (Luke 2. 7). There are three possibilities. The courtyard of an eastern inn, or khan, was surrounded by a series of alcoves with stalls for the cattle, and it may be that Jesus was placed in one of these. But it is also possible that He was born in a " house " (see Matt. 2. 11). The floor of a one-roomed Palestinian house was often on two slightly different levels, and there were mangers by the side of the lower floor, on to which the cattle were driven at night.

There is also a very early tradition that the Lord was born in a cave, used as a shelter for cattle. As Bethlehem is built on a steep limestone ridge the cave could have been part of, and beneath, one of the houses. We saw a number of houses in Bethlehem of this kind, one at the side of Manger Square itself. As early as A.D. 150 Justin Martyr referring to the birthplace of Christ quotes Isaiah 33. 16 in these words, " He shall dwell in a lofty cave of a strong rock " (*Dialogue with*

Trypho, chapter **70**). According to Origen and Jerome, even before Justin's time a particular cave in Bethlehem was venerated by Christians as the birth-place of Christ.

Jerome, a monk who lived here in the fourth century A.D., tells how the emperor Hadrian, in order to try to blot out the remembrance of Christ, planted over the grotto of the Nativity a grove sacred to Adonis. But in A.D. 336 the grotto came to light when Helena the wife of the emperor Constantine built over it a beautiful basilica—the Church of the Nativity. Damaged by fires and the Samaritan revolt, this church was rebuilt under the emperor Justinian (A.D. 528–565), who gave it the form seen today. The soldiers of Chosroes of Persia who in the year 614 destroyed the other churches in the Holy Land spared this one on seeing the mosaics of the Wise Men in Persian dress. Some ancient mosaics of the original church built by Queen Helena can still be seen beneath wooden trap-doors, which are drawn up for the benefit of visitors.

The Church of the Nativity today is an impressive building, not unlike a castle or fortress in appearance; and to enter this, the oldest Christian church in all the world, is to step right into the ancient world of Byzantium. The spacious building with its long double lines of Corinthian pillars, the massive beams made from cedars of Lebanon, and the centuries-old mosaics leave an abiding impression on the visitor. The church is now shared by Greek Orthodox, Latin and Armenian communities; and is encircled by the high walls of their three convents. The tiny entrance looking across the outer court-yard towards Manger Square was made about A.D. 1500—to stop people entering the sanctuary on horseback! An adult has to stoop in order to enter this low doorway; but a child can walk through quite easily.

From the basilica two stairways lead down into the grotto, thirteen steps below the eastern end of the nave. The rude cave, forty feet by sixteen, and ten feet high, is now paved and walled in places with marble, and lit by numerous hanging lamps of silver and gold. In the floor a silver star claims to

9. *Harbour at Caesarea*

10. *Ain Karim in the hill country of Juda, birthplace of John the Baptist*

11. *Road to Bethlehem*

12. *Manger Square, Bethlehem*

3. *Mausoleum at Hebron, built by Herod the Great over the Tombs of the Patriarchs*

4. *River Jordan, traditional place of Our Lord's Baptism*

15. *"A certain blind man sat by the way side begging." Before St. Stephen's Gate, Jerusalem*

mark the exact spot of the Nativity, and bears the inscription in Latin—" Here Jesus Christ was born of the Virgin Mary ". To the right is the place of the manger, in front of which is an altar dedicated to the Magi. The place is full of sacred and tender recollections, although one feels that the marble and tapestries, the silver and the gold, are out of keeping. How much better to have left exposed the bare rock, in order to call forth our devotion to Him Who, though He was rich, for our sakes became poor.

From one end of the grotto a passage leads to several sub-terranean chapels, in one of which Jerome lived for over thirty years and translated the Hebrew and Greek Scriptures into Latin. This version, the Vulgate, was the only Bible our land possessed for many hundreds of years, until Wycliffe, Coverdale and the other translators gave us the Word of God in our own speech. On the morning of Christmas Day, the B.B.C. usually broadcasts the bells of Bethlehem. We climbed the bell tower, and had a fine view across the white houses with their flat roofs, and of the larger buildings a number of which are Christian schools and institutions. It was a perspiring climb as the sun beat down from a sky without clouds, but we tried to do justice to " Ding, dong, merrily on high ", the carol we had so often sung on wintry nights at home.

VI

Away to the south-east of Bethlehem are the Shepherds' Fields, further from the little town itself than is perhaps generally realized. There are no " fields " as such close by, but only cultivated terraces that fall steeply away into the valley. We decided to walk down the road to Beit-Sahur, the shepherds' village; although if you are in a hurry, you can go by bus. Bus tickets in Bethlehem—how incongruous it seems, to travel by bus the journey the shepherds made that first Christmas night! But we enjoyed the walk, in company with a group of laughing school-children, and noticed on the way the boundary stones, or landmarks, between the fields. " You shall not remove your neighbour's landmark, which the men

D

of old have set ", was the command of Deut. **19**. 14. Were these the fields that once belonged to Boaz (Ruth. **2**. 3)? Was it near here that Jesse sent one of his sons to fetch David from keeping the sheep (1 Sam. **16**. 11)?

Near Beit-Sahur there are various chapels and caves in the hill-side associated in one way or another with the shepherds. There are at least three such places! The one we preferred belongs to the Y.M.C.A., and perhaps we liked it best because, feeling tired and very hot—after waiting forty-five minutes for the kettle to boil—we were welcomed with a cup of English tea.

It was not in the chapels, however, that we wanted to linger, but out in those fields where once the light of heaven shone and the herald angels told the news of Messiah's birth (Luke **2**. 8–16). From here the shepherds ran up—and it is quite a steep ascent—to Bethlehem to see and worship the new-born King. Inevitably the words of well-known and well-loved carols flooded through our minds, together with the familiar melodies of Handel's *Messiah*. And, as we looked away beyond the fields, there in the distant background we saw a curiously shaped mountain, rather like a volcano with the top of the cone removed. It reminded us of another and very different king. For the Herodium, or Mount of the Franks, is the burial-place of Herod the Great. Traces can still be seen of the fortress that Herod built there. It was only when the tyrant was dead and buried that the true King he had sought to kill could be brought back from Egypt to the Holy Land (Matt. **2**. 19, 20).

VII

We were often in the little cave of the Nativity. We liked to go there to meditate and pray. One afternoon we met there a professional photographer, a citizen of Jordan from Jerusalem, and remarked how glad we would be if he would take photographs of us kneeling at the spot where our Saviour was born. He said he would be delighted; he would take them on our camera, so that the pictures would be there for us when we arrived back in England. He went to much trouble, screwing and unscrewing bits of apparatus, taking the pictures that we sought.

"And now," we said, "please tell us how much we are in your debt. You have used your bulbs. This is your livelihood. How much do we owe?" "Nothing," he said, "it is my pleasure!" We reasoned with him, but could see that he meant what he said. He would take no money. How far removed all this from the sordid commercialism that goes to make up so much of our western Christmas. The charm of our Arab friend, his generosity, all seemed so right—in Bethlehem, the place where "God so loved the world that He gave . . ."

CHAPTER FIVE

THE WAY TO HEBRON

I

WE SAW IN the last chapter how that just beyond Rachel's Tomb, on the way from Jerusalem to Bethlehem, the road divides. To the left the long sweeping curve leads to Bethlehem itself; to the right a good motor road branches off to Hebron, some twenty-two miles south of Jerusalem.

The road to Hebron keeps fairly close to the watershed of the Judean hills. Away to the east stretches the barren wilderness of Jeshimon, dropping steeply down towards the Dead Sea (1 Sam. 23. 19). While not entirely uninhabited, the few scattered villages in this land of sheep and goats are evidence of the barrenness of the soil. It was in this part of the country, only a few miles south of Bethlehem, that Amos of Tekoa " a herdsman, and a dresser of sycamore trees " was taken by the Lord " from following the flock ", to become the first of the long line of writing prophets (Amos 7. 14, 15).

West of the road the land is more fertile, with villages and

towns more frequent; and the olive, the vine, wheat and summer fruits are grown.   The ancient highway which passes between the brown hills and the fields of countless stones and
hard-won crops is today still used by flocks of sheep, herds
of goats, and trains of camels.   In these days, however, the
shepherd must be prepared suddenly to be startled by the hoot of
a horn, and overtaken by the latest European or American car.

Along this same road centuries ago, after his separation from
his nephew Lot, came the patriarch Abraham, leading *his* sheep,
goats and camels, to sojourn for a while at Hebron (Gen. **13**. 18).
And travelling in the opposite direction, Abraham's great-
grandson Joseph, clad in his garment of long sleeves, the
" coat of many colours ", trudged " from the valley of Hebron "
to visit his jealous shepherd brothers who were then at Shechem
(Gen. **37**. 14).   Along the same road the soldiers of David and
Joab marched northwards to capture the Jebusite fortress at
Jerusalem (2 Sam. **5**. 1–10).   Down this road, his long hair
streaming in the wind, galloped the young prince Absalom, to
raise the standard of revolt in Hebron against his father King
David (2 Sam. **15**. 7–12).   And one far greater than Abraham
or David, lying an infant in the arms of his mother Mary, passed
this same way to Egypt (Matt. **2**. 13, 14).

II

We follow the historic road to Hebron, peopled by the
memories of these great figures of the past, and after nearly
eight miles come upon the famous " Pools of Solomon ".   The
broken-down fortress, more recently used as a *khan*, was built in
the seventeenth century to guard the Pools, but the three large
reservoirs date back to ancient times.   Now filled with bluish-
green water, and situated in a fertile green valley, they have
long been used to supply Jerusalem with water.   As the name
implies, they are believed to date back to King Solomon, perhaps because of the words in the book of Ecclesiastes, " I made
great works; I built houses and planted vineyards for myself;
I made myself gardens and parks, and planted in them all kinds
of fruit trees.   I made myself pools from which to water the

forest of growing trees " (Eccles. **2**. 4–6). Is there a further reference to this fertile area in Song of Solomon **4**. 12, 13, "A garden locked is my sister, my bride . . . an orchard of pomegranates with all choicest fruits "?

Water is always greatly prized in the Holy Land, and we stopped to watch the women with their water-pots, an endless procession making their way down the little side road to the Pools. The scene was repeated some ten miles or so further on, when we paused for a few moments by a spring and cistern of water said to be the place where the evangelist Philip baptized the Ethiopean eunuch. Was this then the way " towards the the south . . . the road that goes down from Jerusalem to Gaza . . . a desert road " (Acts **8**. 26)? Again the water-pots, and the huge, bladder-like black water-skins. An Arab nomad had tethered his heavily-burdened camel in the heat of the day. While he and his veiled wife squatted by the cistern, his four little sons were splashing in the clear, cool water.

III

Hebron itself is situated in a valley surrounded by rocky hills. The valley runs from north to south, and the main quarter of the town lies on the eastern slopes. It is the highest town in Judah, 3,300 feet above sea level. Built " seven years before Zoan in Egypt " (Num. **13**. 22), it was claimed by the Jewish historian Josephus to be the oldest city in the whole of Palestine. It remains today an important centre of communication, for here the north–south road from Jerusalem and Bethlehem to Beersheba and the southern Negeb is crossed by the west–east road from the Maritime Plain to the Dead Sea.

The town is well supplied with water, and is famed for its groves of olive and fruit trees. Its luxuriant vineyards supply the finest grapes. The spies sent out from the wilderness by Moses came to the valley of Eschol, which is just outside and to the north of Hebron, " and cut down from there a branch with a single cluster of grapes, and they carried it on a pole between two of them " (Num. **13**. 23). In Hebron the houses, built of stone, have either flat or domed roofs—often a combination of both.   The town now is one of the largest cities of modern Jordan, with a population of nearly forty thousand.   Only Amman, Jerusalem and Nablus exceed it in size.

The two most famous sites at Hebron are both associated with the patriarch Abraham.   After leaving Lot in the region of Bethel "Abram moved his tent, and came and dwelt by the oaks (or terebinths) of Mamre, which are at Hebron; and there he built an altar to the Lord " (Gen. **13**. 18).   It was while sitting beneath these oaks " at the door of his tent in the heat of the day " that the Lord appeared to him (Gen. **18**. 1).   Seeing three men approaching him, with characteristic eastern courtesy he urged them to accept his hospitality, only to discover later that he was entertaining angels unawares (Heb. **13**. 2). The actual site of Mamre is uncertain, for all that Scripture tells us is that " the cave of the field of Machpelah " (which we shall visit later in this chapter) lay " east of Mamre " (Gen. **23**. 19).

As far back as the time of the emperor Constantine in the fourth century A.D., a large oak tree two miles north of Hebron was venerated as Abraham's oak.   And now for many centuries a large and extremely ancient oak, or terebinth, one and a half miles west of Hebron has been known as the Oak of Mamre.   Today it is surrounded by high railings for protection; parts are covered by an ugly shed, and some of the larger boughs are supported by iron bars.   Although the structure looks decayed, and some of the branches are dead, the tree is still alive, and is cared for by the nearby Russian Orthodox Church.   Was this the place where Abraham entertained the angels?   We cannot be certain.   An Arab student studying his books beneath a clump of trees nearby assured us that beyond all doubt this was the very tree alongside which Abraham had pitched his tent!   It certainly was very old.   In the fierce heat of the day we were glad of the offer of shade, and looked enviously at a party of Jordanian soldiers, who like ourselves had come to see the tree, and who, as they leaned up against the railings, were sucking ice lollies.

IV

" The cave of the field of Machpelah east of Mamre " belonged in Abraham's time to Ephron the Hittite.   When his
wife Sarah died, Abraham spoke to the Hittites, " I am a
stranger and a sojourner among you; give me property among
you for a burying place, that I may bury my dead out of my
sight " (Gen. **23**. 4).   The story which follows in the Book of
Genesis is an exquisite example of oriental bargaining and
courtesy.

The Hittites offer " the mighty prince " the choicest of their
sepulchres, but he desires to possess a family tomb of his own.
Bowing before them he requests the elders to ask Ephron to sell
to him the cave of Machpelah " for the full price ".   Overhear-
ing the request, Ephron generously offers to give it to Abraham;
but in the end agrees to sell it, and the field in which it is
situated, for " four hundred shekels of silver ".   This was the
very first plot of the Holy Land ever to be possessed by the
Hebrews; and in this tomb not only Sarah, but Abraham (Gen.
25. 9), Isaac (Gen. **35**. 29), Rebecca, Leah and Jacob were all
buried (Gen. **50**. 13).

The Haram, or sacred area around the cave, is one, of the
holy places of Islam.   The enormous block-like stones of this
rectangular structure reminded us at once of the Wailing Wall
at Jerusalem (see page 91); for, like the Temple, this was one of
the buildings constructed by Herod the Great.   It stands forty
feet high, but above the Herodian masonry are walls of more
recent construction with lofty minarets.   The Islamic mosque
is almost certainly the remains of an eleventh century church,
at which time there was a bishopric at Hebron.

Until fairly recently, entry into the mosque was forbidden to
those who were not Moslems, but that regulation has now been
relaxed.   We walked in the blinding sun across the great open
courtyard; then, taking off our shoes, entered through the
porchway into the cool, carpeted mosque.   Six large cenotaphs
were pointed out, built well above the caves where the patriarchs
are said to be buried—the cenotaphs of Abraham, Isaac and

Jacob, and of Sarah, Rebecca and Leah. We were invited to peer through a grating in the floor of the building, into the rocky cavern beneath; but if the contradiction be permitted, all that could be seen was darkness. There is an iron door said to lead down to the cave, but so far as is known, no one has entered the actual tomb since the time of the Crusaders.

V

We came out of the cool, quiet of the mosque into the glare of the courtyard. The peddlers were quick to see us and dash across with their wares—postcards, pieces of pottery, and delicate little vases of blue-green Hebron glass. They led, indeed almost dragged us, to the stalls where more of these things were on display. We were taken beneath an archway into a little workshop where we saw the potter at work, and our thoughts turned to Jeremiah, " I went down to the potter's house, and there he was working at his wheel " (Jer. **18**. 3). It was fascinating to see the moist clay spinning round, taking shape at the skilful touch of the potter. And what a selection of pots and vessels there were in the shop, all shapes and sizes from the tiniest dwarfs to veritable giants!

Talking of giants reminds us that Hebron used to be called " Kiriath-arba (the city of Arba); this Arba was the greatest man among the Anakim " (Josh. **14**. 15). When the spies sent out by Moses came to Hebron, "Ahiman, Sheshai, and Talmai, the descendants of Anak, were there " (Num. **13**. 22). These were the giants who gave the majority of the spies a sense of inferiority, making them feel like grasshoppers! That is to say, all the spies except Joshua and Caleb. Because Caleb " wholly followed the Lord, the God of Israel ", he had the courage and morale to overcome these three huge men and conquer Hebron (Josh. **14**. 6–15). And the result was that the fields and surrounding villages of Hebron were given by Joshua to Caleb as an inheritance; the city itself was handed to the Levites and became one of the " Cities of Refuge " (Josh. **20**. 7; **21**. 11).

One lingers in ancient Hebron, watching donkeys plod by followed by figures that have stepped from the pages of the

Bible. Thoughts turn to David and David's men. It was
after the death of Saul that " David enquired of the Lord,
' Shall I go up into any of the cities of Judah? ' And the Lord
said to him ' Go up '. David said, ' To which shall I go up? '
And he said, ' To Hebron ' " (2 Sam. **2**. 1). And so for
seven and a half years David reigned over Judah here at
Hebron, before the capture of Jerusalem, and before he became
king of the northern tribes. In this very place six of his sons
were born. It was in the gate of Hebron that Abner, the commander of the house of Saul, was stabbed to death by the
jealous and masterful Joab (2 Sam. **3**. 27). Here, too, David
made a covenant with all the twelve Hebrew tribes, and was
anointed king over all Israel (2 Sam. **5**. 1–5). Hebron was *the*
royal city before Jerusalem.

Our visit will always be associated in our minds with the
hospitality of two Arab-Moslem homes. In the east, the flat
top of the house, reached by an external stone stairway, is a
good place to entertain guests. And there seven of us sat on
low stools, round a low circular table, sipping mint-flavoured
tea. To the west could be seen the clump of trees at Mamre, to
the north the large modern hospital named after the daughter
of King Hussein, to the east the impressive Herodian mausoleum, the tomb of the patriarchs.

The tea-party on the house-top was followed later by a full
evening meal, and overnight hospitality in another Arab home.
In addition to our host and his brother who waited on the
guests, and our host's little son aged five, there were three others
present. The conversation ranged over a wide variety of topics,
but returned again and again to " the Palestine problem ", the
sad, deep tensions that divide men. The centuries roll past, but
the hearts of men remain the same. The Holy Land is still
restless and divided.

We dined from a large, central common dish, piled high with
a mixture of delicacies mostly unrecognizable to the western eye
and palate. No utensils were used for eating, but after the
meals, before coffee, the host's brother brought in a large flat
pan and an earthen vessel of water. As each guest knelt,

extending his hands over the pan, water was poured over them. In a similar manner Elisha had " poured water on the hands of Elijah " (2 Kings **3**. 11). In some Arab homes the mattresses are rolled up during the day and stacked on shelves at the side of the main living-room, behind a curtain. These are then spread out on the floor last thing at night with no sheets or blankets, but just a single thick cover for warmth.

Hebron—hospitality, courtesy, friendship. These three attractive graces were clearly evident in the hearts and homes of those who so graciously welcomed and entertained us. Our minds were led yet again to Abraham of Hebron, the father of the faithful, honoured alike by Jew, Moslem and Christian. He, too, was hospitable to strangers at the Oak of Mamre. He, too, with a natural courtesy had bowed low before the elders in the gate of Hebron. Above all, he was *the* friend, " the friend of God " (James **2**. 23). No wonder the Arabs have called the town after him—El Khalil—the Friend.

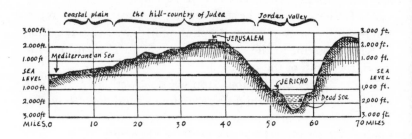

CHAPTER SIX

THE WAY TO JERICHO

I

THE ROAD FROM Jerusalem to Jericho is one of the most remarkable in the world, descending from 2,300 feet above sea level at Jerusalem, to 1,300 feet below sea level at Jericho. One of the best known of our Lord's parables begins, "A certain man went *down* from Jerusalem to Jericho " (Luke **10**. 30, A.V.). The

traveller in the story certainly went *down*.   In some twenty
miles or so the road drops 3,600 feet.   You could free-wheel
most of the way by bicycle, or travel by car without using the
engine at all.   A motorist's paradise?   Not really, for this
highway winds and bends like a serpent, and the driver must
keep continually on the alert.   Passing through desolate mountains and narrow rocky defiles, he must negotiate many sudden
turnings and hair-pin bends.

After leaving Jerusalem and passing round the shoulder of the
Mount of Olives, the view eastward is one of unwelcome desolation.   Rounded barren hills almost devoid of vegetation
(except in spring-time) and rocky gorges fall steeply away to the
Great Rift, the Jordan Valley and the Dead Sea.   There are
few, if any, cultivated fields; only the tents of the Bedouin and
occasional goats and sheep searching for grass.   " Before me,
and all around as far as the eye could follow, blank hills piled
high above hills, pale, yellow and naked, walled up in her tomb
for ever the dead and damned Gomorrah ", wrote Kinglake in
his book *Eothen*.

II

Unlike the man in the parable, we " went down " 'from
Jerusalem to Jericho by car; and our first stop, less than three
miles from the city, was the little Arab village of Al-Azariyeh,
the familiar Bethany of the Gospels.   The present name comes
from the Latin *Lazarium*, the name that was given by Christians
to the village which grew up around the tomb of Lazarus in the
fourteenth century.   Before entering this little village of white,
flat-topped houses we stopped to take pictures of two small
Arab boys with their donkeys—waiting for *baksheesh*.   The
animals reminded us of how Jesus borrowed a donkey at
Bethphage not far away, and rode over Olivet into Jerusalem
(Mark **11.** 1, 2).

New Testament Bethany was probably a little higher up the
slope than the present Arab village, and was the home of
Martha, Mary and Lazarus, where our Lord stayed on a number of occasions (John **12.** 1; see also **11.** 5).   We remember

the welcome He received there during the final dread days before Calvary.   Nobody knows today the exact site of that
friendly home.   In the fourth century, a Byzantine church was
built to commemorate Lazarus and his two sisters, and of this
building part of the apse and mosaic pavement still remain.   A
second church was built not long afterwards; and then a third,
by the Crusaders.   The present Church of St. Lazarus is more
recent—it was erected in 1953—but stands on the foundations of these three older buildings.   It contains four beautiful
mosaic pictures inside and one outside, depicting scenes in
the home at Bethany, and the raising of Lazarus from the
dead.

After enjoying a brief rest in the cool interior of the church,
we went outside and crunched up the rocky path a few yards, to
the alleged tomb of Lazarus.   A little girl, her mother standing
by, was handing out lighted candles and expecting coins.   We
took a candle, stooped and entered the gloom—cautiously
negotiated twenty-four steps down into the rock—just managed
to squeeze through a narrow horizontal aperture—and crouched
in the small cave or mortuary chamber.   It was so eerie, so
quiet, so deep.   Originally the entrance was from the courtyard in front of the church, but when a mosque was built there
in the sixteenth century this entrance was closed.

There is very little evidence that this really was the tomb of
Lazarus, although the place we visited gave new meaning to
the story in John, chapter **11**: " It was a cave, and a stone lay
upon it " (John **11**. 38).   When " the dead man came out, his
hands and feet bound with bandages, and his face wrapped
with a cloth " (John **11**. 44), did he struggle up the steps of a
cavern like this?   No wonder Jesus " cried with a loud voice,
' Lazarus, come out! ' ".   One cannot linger at Bethany without being reminded of the two great truths which our Lord
taught us there: the importance of making time in this busy
world to sit at His feet and listen to His Word (Luke **10**.
38–42); and the truth that to all who trust in Him, He
is both now and hereafter " the resurrection and the life "
(John **11**. 25).

III

Less than five miles from Jerusalem, from the wide sweeping curve in the road we saw to our left the Apostles' Fountain, so called because it is said that, on their way to Jerusalem just before the first Palm Sunday, our Lord and His disciples stopped here for refreshment. They must have been weary indeed by the time they had toiled as far as this. The fountain here, so distant from any other water supply, dates back to Old Testament times, and is identified by some with " the water of En-shemesh " (Josh. **15**. 7), part of the boundary between the territory of the tribes of Judah and Benjamin.

By the Apostles' Fountain the view is attractive and pleasing, and cameras are quickly brought into use. But now the cruel road goes down, down, the heat becomes more intense, and we speed on through ravines and past overhanging rocks, mocked by the burnt-out watercourse alongside. It is not difficult to see why the Lord Jesus chose this road as the setting for His famous parable. He may well have been describing an actual incident, for this is ideal country for highway robberies. Indeed, travel books of only a few years ago make reference to such incidents. The landscape is mountainous and uninhabited, and riddled with caves. It would be easy for robbers to hide behind the crags and massive boulders, since the twists and bends make it impossible for the traveller to see what is lurking round the next corner. The road to Jericho seems designed for sudden ambush. Jerome in the fifth century says that it was known as " the red, or bloody way ". This is " the Ascent of Blood " referred to in the Bible (Josh. **15**. 7; **18**. 17), although the name was given originally because of the exposed patches of red ochre along its course.

We stopped at *Khan Hathrour*, the Inn of the Good Samaritan, which stands at a point about half-way between Jerusalem and Jericho. From ancient times this has been both a caravanserai, or resting-place for travellers, and a police-post from which some sort of control might be exercised over the surrounding desolate country. The present rectangular, one-storied building was rebuilt by the Turks in the last century to provide rest and safety for travellers. We found it partly ruined, and occupied by the Jordan Police and soldiers of the Arab Legion who were camping in tents close by.

A young mounted policeman received us with a smile, and chatted with us about his training and work. We strolled into the courtyard, and stopped by the ancient well. This then was where the wounded traveller was refreshed. Jesus Himself knew the place. So did His hearers. And it was good to linger there and reflect upon the wealth of kindness that has flowed through the world from that lovely story of the Good Samaritan. For it is possible that our Saviour had this very caravanserai in mind when He told how the Good Samaritan brought the wounded traveller " to an inn, and took care of him " (Luke **10**. 34). On such a dangerous and desolate road, as along any of the roads of life, we may meet the neighbour, our fellow-man in need, and loving-kindness can turn " the ascent of Blood " into the King's highway, for He comes to meet us in those who are in need.

IV

Down, down, down. We stopped to photograph the road sign SEA LEVEL; the air became even more oppressive, and we were glad to get moving again. Scanty herds of goats foraged on the mountain-side, and once we saw silhouetted against the sky-line a number of camels. Here and there were the " houses of hair ", the black tents of the Bedouin, who in the heat of the afternoon were quiet and resting. One of the desolate valleys in this locality may have been the Valley of Achor, where Achan was stoned for his disobedience and theft (Josh. **7**. 25, 26),—an ugly, hostile place in keeping with its memories.

And so down to the level plain and " the city of the palms ", Jericho. The present Arab town of Jericho, on the site of both the Byzantine and Crusader Jericho, has a number of beautiful gardens; and, as we passed through, our driver pointed out a sycamore tree, like the one Zacchæus climbed long ago when the Saviour passed through (Luke **19**. 4). However, the

Jericho in which the Lord Jesus brought salvation to the tax-collector and gave sight to blind Bartimæus was sited else-where. That Jericho was built by Herod the Great, and its ruins are nearer to where the road enters the broad plan.

There is yet another and far older Jericho. According to Dr. Kathleen Kenyon, the original Jericho belongs to the Stone Age, somewhere between 8,000 and 10,000 B.C. It is the oldest walled city in the world so far discovered. In the long course of time the ruins of the towns which succeeded one another have built up a " tell " or mound which is about seventy feet high. We walked over the top of this mound, sauntered among the ruins, and went down a considerable distance into the ground to see a little of the excavated wall, guard-room and gateway. Marks made by a fire were plainly visible on the walls at one point. Authorities differ as to whether or not this was the exact site of Joshua's Jericho, but some of the stones on this ancient mound may well have echoed to the clatter of the steps of guards announcing the invasion of Joshua's armies (Joshua, chapter **6**).

We chatted with a swarthy young Arab who told us that he worked for the archæological teams during the winter, but in summer-time, when it was too hot for this kind of work, he sold oranges to visitors. The heat was so intense now that we were glad to buy one of his juicy oranges, for which the Plain of Jericho is famed. Our friend was a refugee, one of the many in this part of the world, whose home was among the shacks of the large settlement that could be seen near to Jericho from the top of the ancient mound. Just beside the Tell, to the east, is " the Fountain of Elisha ", the spring whose bitter waters were made sweet by the prophet's handful of salt (2 Kings **2**. 21). As we passed by, Arab women, shepherds, soldiers and children were washing their hands and faces. Women with the carriage of queens were moving to and fro with water jars balanced on their heads. The donkeys stood listlessly by in the fierce heat.

v

Only a short distance beyond Jericho is the Jordan, a river which meanders for 233 miles from the snow-capped heights of

Hermon down to the Dead Sea. The Jordan forms a barrier rather than a link. Between the Judean hills and the river itself there are pasture lands and cultivated fields, but as the river is approached these give way to the desert-like *qattara*, which cannot be cultivated. Beyond the *qattara* is the *zor*, a narrow strip of jungle, the home of wild beasts, called in the Bible the pride, or " jungle of the Jordan " (Jer. **12**. 5). The swift current, together with these jungle and desert strips, has always presented a formidable barrier.

Somewhere near here the Hebrews under Joshua crossed and invaded the land. A little north of Jericho is the site of Gilgal where they set up the twelve stones after crossing (Josh. **4**. 19, 20). The place where Jesus was baptized is also traditionally located near here, although the Gospels give us no exact indication of the position of " Bethany beyond the Jordan " (John **1**. 28). We stayed at this place as long as we could tolerate the oppressive heat, standing in the shade of a shack to watch the sellers of oranges and drinks, and of little bottles of Jordan water that were being offered for sale to tourists.

The river at the place of baptism was smaller and narrower than we had imagined. The water swiftly moving between willows and tamarisks had a faint green tinge, but was very muddy. No wonder Naaman the proud Syrian general preferred the waters of Abana and Pharpar (2 Kings **5**. 12). Only a narrow river, with steep, slimy, yellow-red banks—yet in such a place the Son of God accepted baptism and dedicated Himself to His vocation as Servant-Messiah. Here " He saw the heavens opened and the Spirit descending upon Him like a dove; and a voice came from heaven, ' Thou art my beloved Son; with Thee I am well pleased ' " (Mark **1**. 10, 11).

Our Lord's baptism was followed immediately by His temptation in the wilderness (Mark **1**. 12, 13). According to ancient tradition His days of fasting took place on the mountain of the Jebel Qarantal, which rises up behind old Jericho. Over halfway up this mountain, and built partly in the solid rock, is the Greek Orthodox monastery said to be built over the grotto where the temptation took place. We had a fine view of this

mountain from Khirbat el Mafgar, a little to the north of
Jericho, when visiting the ruins of the palace of the Umayyad
Caliph Hisham'Abd, who ruled the vast Arab dominion from
India to Spain from A.D. 724–743. These buildings, some of
which have now been excavated, included a palace, a bath, a
mosque, an ornamental pool and a colonnaded forecourt. Here,
too, are to be seen some of the loveliest mosaics in the world.

VI

Not far to the south-east of Jericho the river Jordan flows into
the Dead Sea. We made our way along the western shore of
this desolate stretch of water for some miles to visit the now
famous Qumran caves. It was here that an Arab boy from
Bethlehem, while looking for a stray goat, made one of the most
startling finds of this century, discovering the Dead Sea Scrolls.
To reach Qumran it is necessary to follow an old cart-track,
with continual bumps and ruts, and with no bridges over the
many streams. At one point we all climbed out while the un-
laden car negotiated the stony bed. But we did manage to
visit two of the caves. We saw, too, the monastery of the
Essenes on a hill-top, with the higher Judean mountains rising
up behind. What further treasures are waiting to be discovered
in this desolate region?

We had been looking forward eagerly to a bathe in the waters
of the Dead Sea, and so it was with a sense of relief that we
turned back from Qumran towards the north-western shore.
This remarkable inland sea, forty-three miles long and nine
miles wide, in places more than 1,300 feet deep, lies 1,274 feet
below the Mediterranean, and is the lowest point on the earth's
surface. It is also the most salt-saturated water in the world,
containing about 25 per cent. of solid matter. We were surprised to find in such barren surroundings that this particular
stretch of shore is being developed as a lido, with modern hotels
and restaurants. You can laze there on the beach, sunbathe,
take tea.

To bathe in the Dead Sea is a pleasant and remarkable experience. " But be sure to keep the water out of your eyes and

E

mouth," the café proprietor told us. It is almost impossible to sink. If you rest on your back, your feet and arms and legs pop out of the water like floating corks. You can relax without effort, and the water is pleasantly warm. But you need a thorough shower when you come out, or the thin film of salts will remain to irritate the skin. The view is desolate here, yet not without a compelling beauty. The colour is lovely, with the blue waters, and the mountains of Moab beyond fast reddening in the westering sun. It is widely believed that the extreme southern part of the Sea covers the ruined cities of Sodom and Gomorrah. Here " the Lord rained on Sodom and Gomorrah brimstone and fire from the Lord out of heaven ", and " Lot's wife behind him looked back, and she became a pillar of salt " (Gen. **19**. 24, 26).

We could not help comparing and contrasting the two inland Lakes and Seas, the Sea of Galilee in the north, and the Dead Sea in the South. The one is a symbol of life, the other death. Why this difference? The river Jordan flows into the Lake of Galilee at the north, and flows out again at the south. The same Jordan flows into the Dead Sea further south—but *there is no outlet*. Is not this a parable? If we take in the gifts and resources that God has so freely lavished upon us, but fail to give them out in service and witness, we too will become sterile and barren.

CHAPTER SEVEN

(1) THE WAY TO SAMARIA: JERUSALEM TO SYCHAR

I

JESUS " LEFT JUDEA and departed again to Galilee. He had to pass through Samaria. So he came to a city of Samaria, called Sychar " (John **4**. 3–5). It was typical of the Lord Jesus that He should take that direct way home. Jews travelling from

Judea to Galilee usually went eastwards down to Jericho and, after crossing the Jordan, travelled northwards through Perea. This was a long and roundabout route, but in this way they managed to avoid crossing the territory of the despised, heretical and hated Samaritans. Free of all such racial and sectarian prejudice, the Saviour took the shorter and direct way to Galilee through a territory rich in Biblical associations. In this chapter we shall follow in His steps along the King's highway from the holy city to Jacob's Well at Sychar.

II

First of all, just a little about the territory through which we pass as a whole. Soon after the death of King Solomon, the Hebrew kingdom was divided, and Rehoboam, Solomon's son, was left to rule over Judea (in the south) only. Under the leadership of Jeroboam the ten northern tribes broke away from the House of David (1 Kings 11. 26). Among these ten tribes, Ephraim and Manasseh (the two sons of Joseph) were outstanding in power, influence and leadership, so much so that some of the prophets actually refer to the whole northern kingdom as Ephraim. It is through the territory of these two tribes that we shall be travelling in this and the following chapter.

As we are still in the central highlands of Palestine, the scenery does not differ greatly from that of Judea. But the landscape is generally more pleasant in appearance, and the soil, especially in the valleys, is more fertile. The road winds through hills dotted with villages, some of which stand on or near the sites of Biblical towns whose names are known throughout the Christian world. The fertile valleys, vividly green in the spring, contrast with the surrounding rocky limestone hills. And between the two are the cultivated terraces forming broad steps up the hill-sides. Here are vineyards and olive-yards, and orchards of summer fruits.

But the picture can change swiftly—here a desolate hill-side strewn with countless stones and huge boulders, there a clump of grey-green olive trees; now the reddish-brown soil of a newly ploughed field, then a grassy patch carpeted with tiny brightly-coloured flowers. Truly it was said of Ephraim and Manasseh, " Blessed by the Lord be his land, with the choicest gifts of heaven above . . . with the finest produce of the ancient mountains, and the abundance of the everlasting hills, with the best gifts of the earth and its fulness " (Deut. **33**. 13–16).

III

The road leaves Jerusalem at the Damascus Gate. The present walls and gates of the city were built by the Turks under Sultan Suleiman the Magnificent in the sixteenth century, although the lower courses of the Damascus Gate in the northern wall are dated between the second and fourth centuries A.D. From the seventh century A.D. it was called in Arabic the " Bab el Amud " (gate of the column). According to an early mosaic map, a large column stood on this spot in Byzantine times. This Damascus Gate, a noble piece of architecture, has become the most important centre of the Old City. There are stalls beneath the gate itself, and pictures in older books show a market outside, with the peasants from the surrounding villages displaying their wares. Today, unfortunately, they have been replaced by modern cars, and at the time of our visit the large space in front of the gate was being used as a huge and ugly car park. This impression of modernity remained with us for a short time as we left the gate and began our journey northwards. For the road to Nablus passes first through the most recent part of Jerusalem in Jordan. To left and right are modern shops and hotels, schools and colleges, and the consulates of several foreign countries. We stopped for a while to see the " Tombs of the Kings ", which we shall be visiting again in Chapter Twelve, page 118.

IV

Less than two miles outside Jerusalem we climbed the western slope of Mount Scopus. Here some of the great generals of Biblical history, Assyrian, Babylonian, Roman, drew up their forces for the assault on the city; for Jerusalem, " City of

Peace ", has been ravaged by war and suffering throughout her long history.   Not far to the north-east is Anathoth, the home of the prophet Jeremiah (Jer. **29**. 27), and two miles further to the north is a cone-shaped hill which marks the site of Gibeah of Benjamin.   This is the place where Saul the first king of Israel had his royal residence.   On one occasion he is described as " sitting at Gibeah, under the tamarisk tree on the height, with his spear in his hand, and all his servants were standing about him " (1 Sam. **22**. 6).   Near here, too, stood Gibeon, where the crafty Gibeonites made their league with Joshua (Josh. **9**. 3–15). In his vigorous description of the Assyrian advance on Jerusalem, Isaiah gives the names of quite a number of the little towns which stood on or near this central route in his day (Is. **10**. 28–32).

Here we are on the often disputed border between the two ancient Hebrew kingdoms, which was only five miles north of Jerusalem.   Ramah, the birthplace of the prophet Samuel, stood right on this frontier (1 Sam. **1**. 1); it belonged now to Israel, now to Judah.   Through this town the chained captives of Jerusalem went weeping, on their journey to distant Babylon; and here it was that Jeremiah was freed from his chains and set at liberty (Jer. **40**. 1).   Just a little beyond Gibeon, descending westwards into the valley, ran the old Roman road to Antipatris and to the capital Cæsarea, the city we visited in Chapter Three, page 38.   It is probable that Peter reached the Plain of Sharon by this road, and we recalled how its stones once echoed to the tramp of the two hundred soldiers, seventy horsemen and two hundred spearmen who escorted Paul to the governor (Acts **23**. 23–33).

v

But all that was long ago—and our minds were brought back to the twentieth century by an interruption to our journey. There was in fact a traffic queue on this ancient highway.   We had reached Kalandia airport, about five miles from the attractive modern town of Ramallah.   King Hussein of Jordan had been visiting Nablus and was now returning to Amman by plane. The modern airstrip crosses the ancient road, and so primitive farm carts, drivers with their animals, drooping donkeys and supercilious camels, as well as the latest in taxis and cars, had to wait while the airliner roared along the runway and disappeared over the eastern hills.

Mizpah, the next place along the road, distant about eight miles from Jerusalem, was excavated in 1932–35. It was the first political centre in the Promised Land. Here Samuel gathered the people for reformation, and here Saul was elected king (Jud. **20.** 1; 1 Sam. **7.** 5; **10.** 17). It became the administrative centre of Palestine following the destruction of Jerusalem by the Babylonians in 586 B.C. At Mizpah Jeremiah lived with the governor Gedaliah, until the rebel Ishmael and ten associates killed the governor and seventy of his loyal supporters, and forced the prophet to accompany them to Egypt— where, according to tradition, he was martyred. Archæologists claim to have discovered the pit into which the seventy slain men were cast (Jer. **41.** 1–9). Beyond Mizpah is Bireh, the ancient Beroth. As this was the first caravan halt from Jerusalem to Galilee, it could have been the place where Joseph and Mary first discovered that the boy Jesus was missing from their party. The place of the *khan* where they stayed is still pointed out. "Supposing Him to be in the company (his parents) went a day's journey . . . and when they did not find Him, they returned to Jerusalem, seeking Him" (Luke **2.** 44, 45). A fine spring still flows near Bireh.

VI

Centuries ago these central highlands were visited by the nomadic patriarchs Abraham and Jacob. The road passes quite near to Bethel over in the hills to the right, Bethel so prominent in the pages of the Old Testament. Abraham pitched his tent between Bethel and Ai, and there built an altar for the worship of God (Gen. **12.** 8; **13.** 3). The sun beat down upon us as we stood looking at Bethel in the hills, and remembered how, long ago, Jacob fleeing northwards from the wrath of his brother Esau, spent the night just there with the earth as his bed and a stone for his pillow. Here in his dream he saw the stairway reaching up from earth to heaven, and heard the voice of God with the promise that he would inherit this land (Gen. **28.** 10–22). Because Jacob had found that Bethel was " none other than the house of God, and the gate of heaven ", it later became a famous sanctuary, a centre of religious life, visited by Samuel, Elijah and Elisha. But Jeroboam the founder of the northern kingdom, desirous of finding for his people a substitute for the worship of the Jerusalem temple, set up " a golden calf ", a bull idol, here and at Dan (1 Kings **12.** 33). Here Amos came to protest in God's name against the idolatry and vice of the northern kingdom, undaunted by the fact that it was " the king's sanctuary " (Amos **7.** 13).

To pass on from Bethel to Shiloh, which is about twenty-three miles from Jerusalem, is to pass in thought from Jacob and Amos to Eli and Samuel. Seiloun, to the right of the road, is the ancient Shiloh, where the " ark of God " remained for about three centuries, in what appears to have been a solid sanctuary or temple—for it is described as a " house " with doors (1 Sam. **3.** 15). Here " the boy Samuel was ministering to the Lord under Eli ", and heard the voice of God calling him to the prophetic ministry. Probably the sanctuary was destroyed by the Philistines after the capture of the Ark, and Shiloh then sank into neglect and ruin (Jer. **7.** 12).

We continued northward, following the winding road, watching isolated peasant farmers toiling in their fields, occasionally passing tiny villages, and being passed by ostentatious modern cars. There were several valleys to be crossed. The most beautiful of these was the Valley of Lebonah, a few miles beyond Shiloh, where we stayed for a while to enjoy the vivid green of the springing crops. Here was once an important caravanserai, standing on the boundary between Judea and Samaria in the days of our Lord. By stopping here for the night, Jews travelling northward could pass right through Samaria without having to sleep in that hated land. Here too, in this valley, the grapes were grown from which the Jerusalem temple was supplied with wine. Turning the pages of our Bibles, we found it

interesting to note how some of these places we had just passed
are located there with reference to one another—Judges **21**. 19,
for example: " Behold, there is the yearly feast of the Lord at
Shiloh, which is north of Bethel, on the east of the highway that
goes up from Bethel to Shechem, and south of Lebonah."

VII

Soon after leaving the Valley of Lebonah, we could discern in
the distance the holy mountain of Gerizim which rises above the
plain of Mukhnah.   But before entering the valley between the

two mountains of Gerizim and Ebal to visit Nablus, we turned
off the road a little to the right to see Jacob's Well, the place
where our Lord met the woman of Samaria.   It is not always
possible to identify Biblical sites in the Holy Land with complete certainty—but of this one there can be no doubt.   Jacob,

Joseph buried at Shechem

following in the footsteps of his grandfather Abraham, had settled for a time at Shechem (near which the town of Nablus now stands) and had acquired the land on which he pitched his tent (Gen. **33**. 18, 19). There he dug a well; and at his death, he bequeathed this plot of land to Joseph his son (Gen. **48**. 22; John **4**. 5), who after the Hebrews left Egypt was himself buried at Shechem (Josh. **24**. 32).

The visitor today, who expects to see this well in the open air surrounded by a garden or trees, or perhaps at the road-side, will be disappointed. It is located in the dark crypt of a church, surrounded by gloomy ikons and guttering candles. At the end of the fourth century, a Byzantine church, a few remains of which can still be seen, was built over the well. Damaged by the Samaritans and restored by Justinian (A.D. 528–65), it later fell into decay. The Crusaders built another church, the choir of which stood over the crypt containing the well. This was destroyed in 1187. In 1860 the Greek Orthodox Church gained possession of these ruins, restored the crypt and in 1914 *began* the restoration of the Crusaders' church. " Which of you, desiring to build a tower, does not first sit down and count the cost, whether he has enough to complete it? " (Luke **14**. 28). The owners, not having heeded this warning, have left a half-built church on the site for over half a century.

We sat down to read the story from John's Gospel, chapter **4**. Somebody looked at his watch, and noticed that it was exactly noonday! "Jacob's well was there, and so Jesus, wearied as he was with his journey, sat down beside the well. It was about the sixth hour." So we read on . . . until it was time to descend and see the well itself. Within the walls of the unfinished church stand two unimpressive structures not unlike decrepit builders' huts. They cover two stone stairways down into the crypt, which encloses the ancient well. Here, in spite of the unnatural surroundings, we felt that we were indeed standing on holy ground. Just here " the Saviour of the world ", wearied by his long walk from Judea, had sat down. The priest in attendance let down the pail, and then wound it up brim full of clear, cold water. To drink it, as we all did, was like drinking from the cup of Holy Communion, for we felt aware of the presence of Christ and the water seemed sacramental. Were these the very stones His eyes beheld? Was this the well-side where He rested? When we had finished drinking, the priest filled a small cup with the water and threw it down the well. We waited in hushed silence for what seemed many seconds before we heard the splash of the water in the bottom. And we remembered that the Samaritan woman had said to Christ, " Sir, the well is deep " (John 4. 11).

On coming up from the crypt and looking about us, we were impressed by the nearness of Mount Gerizim, upon which the temple of the Samaritans had once stood. How easy it had been for the Samaritan woman to point to it as she said, " Our fathers worshipped on *this* mountain; and you say that in Jerusalem is the place where men ought to worship" (John 4. 20). Looking between the trees in a more northerly direction, we could see on the slope of Mount Ebal the white, flat-topped houses of the little hamlet of 'Askar, the Biblical Sychar, from which the woman had trudged in the heat of noonday to draw water. Sitting on the rim of the well, Christ would have seen the people of this village walking down to meet him—souls ripe for the harvest.

Sitting there in the shade of the trees just outside the half-built church, these great truths came flooding into our minds. " Everyone who drinks of this water will thirst again, but who-ever drinks of the water that I shall give him will never thirst; the water that I shall give him will become in him a spring of water welling up to eternal life . . . The hour is coming when neither on this mountain nor in Jerusalem will you worship the Father . . . God is spirit, and those who worship Him must worship in spirit and truth . . . Lift up your eyes, and see how the fields are already white for harvest." For the traveller on every road, Christ Himself is the water of life; in every place we may worship God through Him; at every season there is a harvest to be reaped for Him. No wonder the Samaritans con-fessed, " We know that this is indeed the Saviour of the world."

CHAPTER EIGHT

THE WAY TO SAMARIA: (2) SYCHAR TO SEBASTE

I

THE SMALL FERTILE plain in which Jacob's Well is situated is like the hub of a wheel from which the ancient roads, the spokes, radiate outwards. A little to the west, the plain is dominated by the two sacred mountains Ebal and Gerizim. Between them, the road we are now to follow runs westwards to the Mediterranean Sea and then divides, so that a branch runs northwards to Galilee. Eastwards there is easy communication by the Wadi Farah with the Jordan Valley, and over the Damiyeh Ford (thought by some to be near the ancient Adam of Josh. 3. 16, where the waters were cut off) to trans-Jordan. There is thus a highway right across Samaria from the Mediterranean Sea to the Jordan. This east–west route crosses the main south–north route from Jerusalem to Galilee in the little plain where the well is situated, near to which stood the Biblical city of Shechem. If Jerusalem is the spiritual, this is the geographical centre of the Holy Land—the hub of the King's highways.

We stayed to rest a little while at Jacob's Well, in the shade afforded by the walls of the half-built church, and then continued our journey, turning westwards towards the pass between Mount Ebal and Mount Gerizim. The mid-day sun was beating down from a cloudless sky. We stopped for a little while to admire the wares of a potter, and chat with a group of Arab boys from the nearby refugee camp, who were selling oranges. Less than a mile from Jacob's Well is the small, and rather dirty, village of Balata. The name is derived from the Aramaic *Ballout*, which means " oak ".

This is the traditional site of the sacred terebinth or oak, supposed by the ancient Canaanites to give oracles. "Abram passed through the land to the place at Shechem, to the oak of

Moreh " (Gen. **12.** 6).   His grandson Jacob, who also lived for
a time at Shechem, took the foreign gods of his household and
" hid them under the oak which was near Shechem " (Gen. **35.**
4).   Close by this village is the partly excavated Tell Balata,
the site of ancient Shechem; and in these excavations, the base
of " the Tower of Shechem " which was destroyed by Abimelech,
one of the Judges of ancient Israel, has been revealed (Judges
9. 46–49).   Rehoboam, son of Solomon, was crowned at Shechem and it was here that the foolish young king brought about
the disruption, the division of the kingdom into Judah and
Israel.   " Then Jeroboam," the leader of the rebellion that led
to the split, " built Shechem in the hill country of Ephraim, and
dwelt there " (1 Kings **12.** 25).   This means that he fortified it
as his capital.

But although it was an excellent centre of communications,
as we saw at the beginning of this chapter, it was not a good
defensive position, and Jeroboam soon decided to shift his
capital to Tirzah, several miles to the north-east (1 Kings **14.**
17; **15.** 21).   Perhaps it was for this same reason that, when
Shechem was destroyed by the Jewish ruler John Hyrcanus in
128 B.C., it was eventually rebuilt by the Romans a little further
to the west.   They then called it Flavia Neapolis, a name which
the Arabs corrupted to Nablus.

II

Today, Nablus with a population of nearly 43,000, is the
third city of the Kingdom of Jordan, second only to Amman
and Jerusalem.   We arrived there on the very day that King
Hussein was making an official visit.   All along the route we
had passed under arches decorated with branches, which reminded us of those " leafy branches . . . cut from the fields "
with which an eastern crowd had welcomed a greater King
long ago, with shouts of " Hosanna " (Mark **11.** 8, 9).   The
citizens of Nablus were giving an enthusiastic welcome to their
young king.   We mingled with the surging and cheering people,
all striving to catch a glimpse of the royal visitor.

Immediately after his departure, as the crowd of boys began

to pull down the branches—and the policemen did their best to stop them!—we went into the hotel where the king had been dining. And there, according to the ingrained habit of the British, we managed to get some tea. We liked Nablus, and spent an enjoyable time wandering round the old city with its narrow streets and dark alleys, stopping here and there to look at the shops or watch the craftsmen at their work. The city now has a steadily increasing number of attractive modern buildings, built in European style. It was not, however, only in buildings that we found this combination of old and new. We were able to visit the modern hospital of the Church Missionary Society. Here the healing ministry of the Christ of yesterday, which was a blessing to the people of Samaria, is continued as the Christ of today mediates His healing power and tender love through his servants.

III

Nablus is built in the narrow valley, the pass between the two sacred mountains. Ebal rises to the north, Gerizim to the south. This was the first place of assembly of all the tribes of Israel at the time of the conquest under Joshua. He " built an altar in Mount Ebal to the Lord," and there " he wrote upon the stones a copy of the law of Moses." The Ark of God stood in the valley with the priests and the people on either side, " half of them in front of Mount Gerizim and half of them in front of Mount Ebal." And " afterward he read all the words of the law, the blessing and the curse " (Josh. **8.** 30–35).

In the period between the Old and New Testaments, Mount Gerizim took on a new importance; events took place which cast their shadow across the pages of the Gospels. After the Northern Kingdom had fallen to the Assyrians in 722 B.C., the Israelites who had not been taken away into captivity inter-married with the Assyrian colonists to form the mixed race of the Samaritans. Nehemiah and Ezra in their zeal for racial purity rejected the offer of these Samaritans to help with the rebuilding of the Temple at Jerusalem (Ezra **4.** 1–3). The Samaritans never forgave the Jews for this rebuff, and they set

up a rival temple and priesthood on Mount Gerizim about
432 B.C. Although this temple was destroyed by the Maccabean ruler John Hyrcanus in 128 B.C., the Samaritans have
continued to this present time to worship on the same spot. A
week before the Annual Passover, the whole Samaritan community camps out on the top of Mount Gerizim, near the site
of the old temple. On the fourteenth of Nisan the lambs are
slain by white-robed men. The wool is then removed by
scalding, and the lambs are spitted and roasted in a pit. When
they are cooked the Samaritans eat them standing, their loins
girded, their shoes on their feet, staff in hand (Ex. 12. 11).

We were able to visit the Samaritan community, and went
inside their synagogue. We thought of the woman of Samaria
(John 4. 7), the healed leper who was a Samaritan (Luke 17. 16),
and the Good Samaritan of Luke 10. 33. We recalled the word
of Scripture, "Jews have no dealings with Samaritans" (John
4. 9; 8. 48), and remembered again the Master's love to all
men everywhere. Here inside the synagogue we were shown a
scroll of the law, which they claimed was the oldest Bible in the
world, but which scholars say is probably not earlier than the
eleventh century A.D. The cylindrical case was covered with
engraved pictures—which included the temple altar, the Ark
of God and the seven-branched candlestick. The tall priests
looked gauntly picturesque in their red turbans, but they gave
the impression of being more interested in receiving gifts than in
the sacred things of their faith. They knew about "the good
Samaritan" in Christ's parable, and suggested that all the
Christians present would be "good Samaritans" if they gave
generous financial support to the Samaritan people! A tiny
dwindling community, physically weakened by inter-marriage,
and yet regarding themselves as the only true Israel, they are
the pathetic remnant of what Ben Sira the Jew rudely described
as "the foolish folk that dwell at Shechem" (Ecclus. 50. 26).

IV

After leaving Nablus, we continued north-westwards along
the valley called Barley-Vale which leads to Sebaste, the ancient

city of Samaria. But before visiting the site, we stopped for a meal in a shelter adjoining a primitive inn. Women were crowding round a well nearby. Their colourful dresses and waterpots would have made a vivid picture, had they not been so obviously anxious to avoid suspicious-looking cameras. An Arab with a mangy-looking camel was offering rides to tourists, rather like donkey rides on Margate sands. But we were keen to continue our journey, to climb the hill to see the ruins of this famous Old Testament city, founded by Omri, king of Israel, about 880 B.C.

What a magnificent site he chose—how beautiful, and how impressive! It was built on a round isolated hill, a little over 300 feet high. That is why the walls which enriched this hill could be likened by the prophet Isaiah to a wreath of flowers on a reveller's head (Is. **28**. 1). The hill is surrounded and overlooked on three sides by the mountains, but away to the west, twenty-three miles in the distance, the sea is just visible. When Omri chose this site, it was cultivated land, as it has become once again today. Here he built his new capital for the Northern Kingdom and made it almost impregnable. "He bought the hill of Samaria from Shemer for two talents of silver; and he fortified the hill, and called the name of the city which he built, Samaria, after the name of Shemer, the owner of the the hill" (1 Kings **16**. 24). We scrambled through ruins to inspect part of the excavated Israelite wall of Samaria. In this wall one large long stone (called a "stretcher") is placed alongside two smaller stones ("headers"). This is a characteristic of Phœnician work, and reminded us of the close alliance between "the house of Omri" and the Phœnician kings. It was the daughter of one of these kings, Jezebel, wife of Ahab, who secured the support of the court for the worship of the Tyrian Baal (1 Kings **16**. 31, 32), an evil influence which was checked by the heroic stand of Elijah on Mount Carmel (1 Kings **18**. 20, 21).

Samaria, so beautiful still today; Samaria, the city we had known from Sunday School days—the scene of so many dramatic happenings, peopled with colourful characters from the pages of the Old Testament.   We made our way over fallen masonry, and climbed weed-covered mounds.   It was here that Naaman the leper came to visit Elisha the prophet; here, too, that the four lepers sat at the gate (2 Kings 5. 3; 7. 3).   So strong was Omri's city that the sieges of Samaria were always prolonged. Even the Assyrians had to invest it for three years (723–721 B.C.) before they could finally capture and destroy it.

V

Although destroyed by the Assyrians, the city of Samaria was destined to rise again and again, as we were reminded by the imposing ruins still to be seen.   Alexander of Macedon, Ptolemy Lagos of Egypt, Gabinius the Roman, and many others left their mark on Samaria, before it was given by the Roman emperor Augustus to Herod the Great.   Herod rebuilt and fortified it, and renamed it Sebaste, the Greek for Augusta, the name by which it is still known today.   The magnificent Herodian town overflowed the large hill, and according to Josephus had a circumference of about two and a half miles. On the summit of the hill, Herod erected a temple to Cæsar Augustus; the massive steps leading up to this temple can still be seen.   It is said to be built over the ruins of Ahab's palace. Parts of these earlier ruins can be explored, and the guide will even point out where " they washed the chariot by the pool of Samaria, and the dogs licked up his (King Ahab's) blood " (1 Kings 22. 37, 38).   Other columns and remains of the Roman period, and of a Crusader church built on the ruins of a Byzantine church, are in evidence.

It was probably this Herodian Sebaste with its fine public buildings, colonnades and gateways that was visited in New Testament times by the evangelist Philip.   He " went down to a city of Samaria (some MSS read " the city of Samaria "), and proclaimed to them the Christ " (Acts 8. 5).   Acts chapter 8 tells how his mission met with great success, and he was joined by the Apostles Peter and John (verse 14).   The Church had begun on the second stage of the Lord's commission—" You shall be My witnesses in Jerusalem and in all Judea and Samaria and to the end of the earth " (Acts **1**. 8).

VI

Did the Lord Jesus Himself walk this way? When He sat weary by the well at Sychar, He was on His way to Galilee from Jerusalem. There are two possibilities. If He were making for the lake-side and Capernaum, He would most probably have taken the road to the north-east from Jacob's Well. If however, He were returning to Nazareth, it is more than likely that He took the north-west road, which passed close by Sebaste and on to the Plain of Dothan where Joseph had visited his brethren (Gen. **37**. 12–18). As we lingered there among the ruins of Samaria, we could see Dothan away to the north. Probably on more than one occasion the Master walked this road. If so, He had been preceded and was followed by many Biblical characters both good and bad. Wicked men and women—Abimelech, Ahab, Jehu, Jezebel, Herod—came this way; so, too, did great men of God—Abraham, Jacob, Joshua, Elijah, Elisha, Philip, Peter. As Joshua had reminded the people assembled on the slopes of Mount Ebal and Mount Gerizim, there are two ways—the way of life and the way of death. Whatever the road along which we walk, it is character that counts. We can follow in *His* footsteps along the way that leads to life.

F

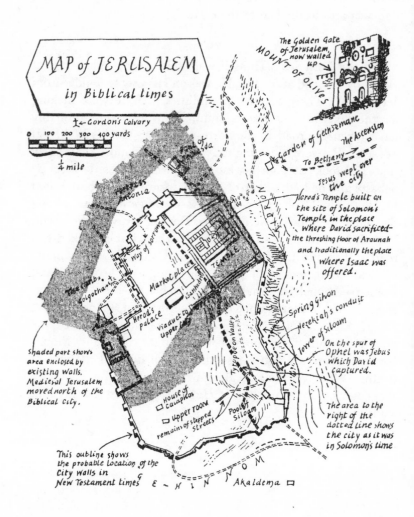

MAP of JERUSALEM

in Biblical times

↑ ← Gordon's Calvary

0 100 200 300 400 yards

¼ mile

The Golden Gate of Jerusalem, now walled up →

MOUNT OF OLIVES

Garden of Gethsemane

To Bethany

The Ascension

Jesus wept over the city

Herod's Temple built on the site of Solomon's Temple, in the place where David sacrificed the threshing floor of Araunah and traditionally the place where Isaac was offered.

Antonia

Way of sorrows

The Tomb"

Golgotha

Market place

Sanhedrin

TEMPLE

Herod's Palace

Viaduct to Upper

KIDRON

Spring Gihon

Hezekiah's conduit

Tower of Siloam

On the spur of Ophel was Jebus which David captured.

Shaded part shows area enclosed by existing walls. Medieval Jerusalem moved north of the Biblical city.

Tyropoeon Valley

House of Caiaphas

Upper room

remains of stepped streets

Pool of Siloam

The area to the right of the dotted line shows the city as it was in Solomon's time

This outline shows the probable location of the City walls in New Testament times

G E - H I N N O M   Akaldema □

PART THREE

Ways in and around Jerusalem

CHAPTER NINE

THE WAY OVER OLIVET

I

" His holy mountain, beautiful in elevation, is the joy of all the earth, Mount Zion . . . the city of the great King." After this lyrical outburst of love and praise for Jerusalem, the Psalmist invites us to " walk about Zion, go round about her " and to " consider well " her walls and buildings (Ps. 48. 2, 12, 13). Perhaps an even better way today of seeing Jerusalem, " the perfection of beauty," is to ascend either the lofty tower of the Y.M.C.A. building, or the tower of the Lutheran Church of the Redeemer which stands close by the Church of the Holy Sepulchre. We plodded slowly up the seemingly endless spiral stairway of the latter (there are 178 steps), but were well rewarded by a magnificent view of the holy city in four directions.

To the south, beyond the present wall, we could make out the rocky spur of Ophel on which the Old Testament city of David originally stood, and also the hill now called Mount Zion. Beyond Ophel to the south-east lay the deep valley of the Kidron, with the Mount of Offence in the background—so called, because it was there that Solomon worshipped his false gods. The Kidron converges with the Valley of Hinnom which runs westwards and then bends northwards. To the west we could see the citadel, and beyond it the new Israeli Jerusalem, with the modern King David Hotel and the imposing Y.M.C.A. building as conspicuous landmarks. To the north, beyond the Damascus Gate, were the modern shops and buildings of Jordan Jerusalem. Looking in this direction, we could see the tower of

the Anglican Cathedral of St. George, Gordon's Calvary behind
the central bus station, and the impressive buildings of the
Archæological Museum.   In this northerly direction there are
no deep valleys, and no natural defence, and it is therefore easy
to see why the fortress of Antonia was built on the northern side.

Eastwards lay the Temple Area, the deep valley of the
Kidron, and the Mount of Olives.   Both sides of the Kidron
Valley are steep; the terrain drops away quickly beyond the
eastern wall of the city until the slopes of Olivet are reached.
In our Lord's day, there was a viaduct stretching across this
valley.   But it is time now to descend our spiral stairway after
this general view of the holy city, and to begin our exploration
of the ways around Jerusalem on this eastern side.

II

" If you wait here for the Jericho bus, you will be in Bethany
in a few minutes."   It seemed strange to be taking a bus to
Bethany—a donkey would have been more appropriate!   But
we waited by the bus stop on the Jerusalem side of the Mount of
Olives, and caught the ramshackle vehicle that bumped along
the Kidron Valley road.   In a little while, the bus turned left,
going eastward, and began to pass round the southern edge of
the Mount of Olives.   It was hot, the travellers were languid,
and the driver-cum-conductor sat over his wheel listlessly
watching the road.   Here and there we passed groups of
Arabs, protected a little by their *kafiyehs*, sitting in whatever
shade they could discover.

We soon reached Bethany, some three miles distant from
Jerusalem by road.   We have already described this village,
the home of Martha, Mary and Lazarus, in Chapter Six.   Our
object now was to walk from Bethany to Jerusalem, over the
Mount of Olives, following the way taken by our Lord on the
first Palm Sunday.   " And when they drew near to Jerusalem,
to Bethphage and Bethany, at the Mount of Olives, He sent two
of His disciples, and said to them, ' Go into the village opposite
you, and immediately as you enter it you will find a colt tied,
on which no one has ever sat; untie it and bring it ' " (Mark

11. 1, 2). Whether the donkey was in Bethany or Bethphage, or in yet a third unnamed village, is not absolutely clear from the Gospels; and the site of Bethphage has never been identified with certainty.

Leaving the main road, we now began to make our way up the track from Bethany towards the summit of the Mount of Olives. " The sun shall not smite you by day " the Psalmist had written (Ps. 121. 6), and while scrambling up this rocky pathway in the afternoon heat it was as though a sword came out and struck us! Some Arabs were amused to see us swelter-ing, and invited us to a shack nearby where they were selling fizzy drinks. We were soon discussing travel, and England, and London; a city, they supposed, where all were prosperous, and whose streets were paved with gold. As we continued our climb, we were at first accompanied by little children looking hopefully for sweets or tips, and some grinning, friendly youths. Still upwards we went past cultivated fields, sun-scorched trees, and an occasional donkey. Rests were welcome, and provided us with opportunities to survey the panorama eastwards. In ranges of differing colours, from deep brown to yellow, the hills could be seen in the foreground; in the distance, beyond the Great Rift were the softer blues of the mountains of Moab. And we remembered how Jesus had often looked at this scene, especially in the course of His visits to Bethany during Holy Week.

III

Near to the broad summit of Olivet the road levels out, and it is most likely that the Biblical Bethphage stood just here. It must have been at this point, therefore, that Jesus mounted the colt for His triumphal entry into the holy city. We left the road in order to visit the church built in 1883, where the Stele of Bethphage, discovered in 1876, is displayed. This stone dates from the Crusader period, and was then revered because it was believed that Christ had stood on it to mount the donkey. On the Stele are pictures of the raising of Lazarus, of the two disciples bringing the colt to Jesus, and of the subsequent procession with palm branches. The name " Bethphage " means " house of unripe figs ", and we wandered over to photograph a clump of fig trees, only a few yards from the track, and quite near to the church. Somewhere about here " when they came from Bethany " and Jesus was hungry, He had approached a fig tree in search of fruit, and " found nothing but leaves " (Mark **11**. 12, 13).

Further along the road and approaching the summit we overtook a flock of sheep, with their distinctive fat tails or " rumps ". We were reminded of several references in the Book of Leviticus, e.g. " Then from the sacrifice . . . he shall offer its fat, the fat tail entire " (Lev. **3**. 9). We shall visit the summit of Olivet in describing the Ascension of our Lord in the final chapter of this book. Our journey now takes us therefore down the western slope towards Jerusalem, turning aside for a brief visit to the church of the Pater Noster (" Our Father "). Luke records the Lord's Prayer immediately after his story of Martha and Mary of Bethany (Luke **10**. 38 to **11**. 4), and perhaps that is the reason for the tradition that Jesus taught His disciples this prayer, for the second time, on the Mount of Olives. The present church of the Pater Noster was built in 1875 over Crusader ruins, and remains of the " Eleona "—the first church built on Olivet by Helena, wife of Constantine in the fourth century A.D. On panels of tiles round the quadrangle the Lord's Prayer is painted in thirty-two languages.

What a wonderful panoramic view of Jerusalem spread out before our Lord as He rode down the western side of the Mount of Olives on that first Palm Sunday! " Let us call to mind the indescribable spectacle of that spring morning, of that brilliant sun climbing up behind Olivet to the crystal-clear sky, and enveloping in its light the splendid city stretching over the opposite hills. The Herodian towers on Mount Zion glowed in the immaculate whiteness of their marbles; lower down, magnificent palaces follow one another in many lines like the various flights of steps of a huge amphitheatre ": this is the description of the Franciscan Guide. The sight of the city there before Him, with all its sacred historic associations, deeply

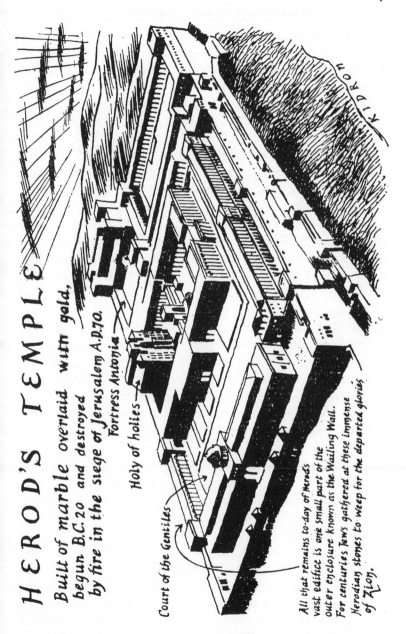

HEROD'S TEMPLE

Built of marble overlaid with gold, begun B.C. 20 and destroyed by fire in the siege of Jerusalem A.D. 70.

Fortress Antonia

Holy of holies

Court of the Gentiles

All that remains to-day of Herod's vast edifice is one small part of the outer enclosure known as the Wailing Wall. For centuries Jews gathered at these immense Herodian stones to weep for the departed glories of Zion.

KIDRON

moved our Lord. Luke tells us, " When He drew near
and saw the city He wept over it " (Luke **19**. 41). This
incident is commemorated by the little church of Dominus
Flevit (" the Lord Wept "), built in 1955 over the remains of an
earlier fifth century church.

It must have been somewhere near here also that the Lord
Jesus " sat on the Mount of Olives opposite the temple ", that
" mountain of marble and gold ", and taught Peter, James,
John and Andrew about the end of the age and His own
personal return (Mark **13**. 3). Sitting there and pondering
that tremendous discourse given on the Tuesday of Holy Week,
we looked down and could see, across the Kidron Valley, the
blocked-up Golden Gate in the eastern wall of the city. This
stands near the site of the former Gate Beautiful (Acts **3**. 2).
The Moslems blocked up this gateway in order, so it is said, to
prevent the Lord Jesus from entering through it in triumph
when He comes again! Again—for it was over the steep of
Olivet that the Lord came riding the first time in lowly majesty
on the first Palm Sunday; " Lo, your King comes to you;
triumphant and victorious is He, humble and riding on an
ass " (Zech. **9**. 9). With waving palm branches and shouts of
" Hosanna ", He passed over Olivet down the steep, rocky
path, across the Kidron Valley and up through the eastern gate
into the courts of the Temple. What did He see there? And
what does the Temple Area look like today?

IV

The Temple Area in the south-east of Jerusalem is sacred to
Jew, Christian and Moslem alike. The large enclosure covers
almost one-sixth of the total area within the city walls, by
which it is bounded on the east and the south. It is called by
the Arabs the Haram es Sherif, the Noble Sanctuary. The
hill on which it stands lay outside the original City of David,
who bought the site, the threshing floor of Araunah the
Jebusite, and " built there an altar to the Lord " (2 Sam. **24**.
18–25). Here, David's son Solomon, with the aid of Hiram of
Tyre, erected the first Temple, where the Hebrews worshipped

for four hundred years, until it was destroyed by Nebuchadnezzar of Babylon in 586 B.C. With the stimulus of the prophets Haggai and Zechariah, the returned exiles rebuilt the Temple on a smaller scale between 520 and 516 B.C.

This modest structure (see Haggai **2.** 3, " Who is left among you that saw this house in its former glory? . . . Is it not in your sight as nothing? ") Herod the Great offered to replace by a magnificent Temple. And so it came about that in the year 20 B.C. Herod began to build the *third* Jewish Temple, in whose courts Christ and the Apostles taught and worshipped. This mighty building was not completed until shortly before its destruction by Titus in A.D 70. It was still unfinished even in our Lord's day; " It has taken forty-six years to build this Temple," said the Jews in John **2.** 20. The site of the second Temple was insufficient for the much larger building Herod had planned. So in order to double the area at his disposal, he constructed enormous vaulted chambers to the south, which are now known as Solomon's Stables. We were keen to explore these vaults, so passing down a flight of steps in the south-eastern corner of the enclosure, we left the blinding sunshine for the cavernous gloom. This dark and damp extensive underground area had obviously been used at one time for stables, since holes had been made in the stones for tethering horses. Whether Herod used and enlarged a cavern made by Solomon is a matter of dispute. The Crusaders probably increased the area, but traces of Herodian stonework certainly remain.

On the enlarged area, Herod built his magnificent Temple of white marble, parts of which were overlaid with gold. The sanctuary was set within a large open space, enclosed by a wall—known as the Court of the Gentiles. From the south-western corner of this court a bridge led westwards into the city; part of the remains of this have been discovered and given the name of " Robinson's Arch ". Within the outer court, and raised fifteen cubits above it, was the Court of the Israelites, to the eastern part of which Israelite women were confined. This was separated from the outer court by a low wall, beyond which no Gentile might pass; "a dividing wall between them", between Jew and Gentile, is the New English Bible translation of Eph. **2**. 14. It was because the Jews thought that Paul had brought a Gentile friend, Trophimus the Ephesian, beyond this separating wall, that they stirred up the riot in the Temple that led to Paul's arrest (Acts **21**. 27–32). Immediately in front of the sanctuary was the Court of the Priests, in which stood the great altar of sacrifice; and beyond a high porch was " the Holy Place " containing the altar of incense, the table of the shewbread and the seven-branched candlestick. Behind the curtain was " the Holy of Holies ", the dark, empty shrine, entered by the high priest only, once a year on the Day of Atonement (Heb. **9**. 7).

V

But this area is sacred to Christians as well as to Jews. It was to Herod's Temple that Joseph and Mary brought the infant Jesus " to present Him to the Lord "; and here at the age of twelve He sat listening to the teachers and asking them questions (Luke **2**. 22, 46). On the eastern side of the Court of the Gentiles, that is, towards the Mount of Olives, there was a portico with a double row of pillars and a roof of wood. It was in this portico, called Solomon's Porch, that Jesus taught, as John records, when He visited Jerusalem in connection with the great festivals (John **10**. 23).

Here also, according to Matthew, Mark and Luke, He taught during the days of Holy Week. Here it was that " teaching daily in the temple " (Luke **19**. 47), He was asked the questions about Authority, the Tribute Money, the Resurrection of the Dead and the Greatest Commandment (Mark **11**. 27 to **12**. 34). Here too, He taught in parables—the Two Sons, the Wicked Husbandmen, the Marriage Supper, and perhaps also the Ten Virgins, the Talents and the Last Judgment (Matt. **21**. 28 to **22**. 14; and chapter **25**). His courageous act in driving out the money-changers and sellers of sacrificial victims from the Court of the Gentiles was an indignant protest against the desecration of the sacred place and the shameless priestly exploitation of the people (Matt. **21**. 12). It may also have been intended as a sign of God's intention to cancel the entire Jewish sacrificial system. It certainly precipitated His arrest and crucifixion.

After the Resurrection, the Apostles and other believers continued for a time to worship in the Temple courts (Acts **2**. 46; **3**. 11; **5**. 12). There, by bold speech and acts of healing, testimony was made to the resurrection and exaltation of Christ. On the north side of the enclosure, at the foot of the present minaret, there was a stairway leading up to the fortress Antonia where Roman guards were constantly on the look-out. Using these steps as a pulpit, Paul, whose life had just been saved by the prompt action of the Roman soldiers, testified to the Risen Lord before the crowd which had attempted to lynch him (Acts **21**. 40). The behaviour of that fanatical mob was symptomatic. The Jews were rushing down a precipice to destruction. On His last visit to the Temple, Jesus had foretold its doom: " Do you see these great buildings? There will not be left here one stone upon another, that will not be thrown down " (Mark **13**. 2).

Just forty years later that prophecy was fulfilled when, amid scenes of indescribable horror, the Temple was destroyed by fire. The fierce, implacable, fanaticism of the Jews had defeated the firm intention of the Roman general Titus to save the Temple. And all that now remains of Herod's vast and imposing edifice is one small part of the outer enclosure. We visited this " Wailing Wall ", as it has come to be called, a number of times, and were impressed by the immensity of the Herodian stones. Here for centuries Jews used to assemble to wail over the destruction of the Temple and the lost glories of Zion. To-day they can no longer visit the Wailing Wall, for it is in the old city, part of the Arab kingdom of Jordan.

VI

Sacred to Jew, Christian and Moslem, we have already said. And what the visitor sees today is an enclosure and buildings devoted to Islam, the Haram es Sherif. In A.D. 638 Jerusalem was captured by the Arabs under the Caliph Omar. His successor, Abdul-Malek, in A.D. 687–691 built the magnificent Dome of the Rock which today dominates the Temple Area, the earliest example of Arabic architecture still in existence. Built on an elevated platform, it is approached up flights of steps, surmounted by arches called Mawazeen or Scales. The mosque itself is octagonal, and above it on a cylindrical drum, the dome rises to a height of 108 feet. The exterior is covered with grey-veined white marble, and the upper part with fine porcelain tiles. The dome, made of plates of aluminium impregnated with gold, gleams in the brilliant sunshine.

On entering through any one of the doors, your eyes at once see *all* the pillars and columns. These are in two concentric rows, the outer row supporting the roof of the outer ambulatory, and the inner one the dome. The area between the two ambulatories, covered with rich Persian carpets, is used for prayer, and can accommodate 3,000 people. Beneath the dome itself, in the centre, is the sacred rock which, massive and gaunt, appears to be suspended in the air. We were now at the very place where for centuries stood the Holy of Holies. We descended beneath the rock into a cave, used as a place of prayer. On this rock, Moslems believe, Abraham was about to sacrifice Isaac (Gen. 22. 1–14), and from it they claim Mohammed ascended into heaven. It was during the Crusader period (A.D. 1099–1187), when the mosque became a Christian church called "Templum Domini", that the rock was surrounded with the present lovely iron grille, to prevent pilgrims chipping off pieces to sell as souvenirs. " Of all public places, it seems to me most worshipful. Chaste and lovely, proportions mellowed by time, its stained-glass glorious, its proportions filling the eye with satisfaction, its atmosphere subdued and reverential, its memories unparalleled, it is the natural place of prayer," writes H. E. Fosdick in *A Pilgrimage to Palestine*.

The other main Moslem building in the area is the El Aqsa mosque, built by Caliph Al-Waleed, son of Abdul-Malek. Only a little of the original mosque remains in the present structure, which has been rebuilt several times and was completely renovated in 1938–42. It is on the south side of the area. We removed our shoes in the porch, where a corpse was lying covered with a cloth, awaiting the hour of prayer, and walked silently over the soft carpets down the central aisle. The building with its snow-white walls and columns looked like a vast, empty Christian basilica. A beautiful pulpit constructed entirely without nails was the gift of Saladin, the great Saracen leader who fought against the Crusaders. Men, including soldiers, were standing or prostrating themselves in the direction of Mecca, before the prayer niche or Mihrab. In the very place where Jesus had stressed the great commandment, " The Lord our God, the Lord is one ", men were chanting, " There is no God but Allah ".

VII

On the occasion of " the Cleansing of the Temple ", the Lord Jesus made a prophecy. " Destroy this temple, and in three days I will raise it up " (John 2. 19). Misunderstood by His hearers, misinterpreted by the malicious, this saying was flung at Him as a bitter taunt as He suffered on the cross, outside the city wall (Mark 15. 29, 30). But the prophecy came true. Herod's magnificent Temple was destroyed and its elaborate sacrificial system ended by the Roman Titus in A.D. 70.

But the Christ Who on the third day rose from the dead is the Head of His Body, the Church—the new universal temple. The old Temple, for all its splendour, was built with dead stones—immense and beautiful, but dead. The new temple is built of living stones " into a spiritual house, to be a holy priesthood, to offer spiritual sacrifices acceptable to God through Jesus Christ " (I Peter 2. 5). So the whole wide earth has become the sacred enclosure, the Temple Area. " The hour is coming, and now is, when the true worshippers will worship the Father in spirit and truth " (John 4. 23). Not in vain did the Saviour ride over Olivet to the Temple. " Blessed be He who comes in the name of the Lord! Hosanna in the highest! "

CHAPTER TEN

THE WAY OF BETRAYAL

I

IN THIS CHAPTER we shall follow in the footsteps of our Lord " on the night when He was betrayed ". The Gospels tell us that the day before the Crucifixion, Jesus sent two of His disciples into the city of Jerusalem to prepare the passover meal in " a larger upper room furnished and ready " (Mark **14**. 15). Here " when it was evening He came with the twelve ", presided at the Last Supper, washed the feet of His disciples, and delivered those wonderful discourses recorded in John's Gospel, chapters **13** to **17**. It is not possible to identify with certainty the exact site of this Upper Room where the Last Supper was held. Ancient tradition locates it on the conspicuous hill, wrongly called Mount Zion, which now lies outside the city wall to the south-west.

When we were in Israeli Jerusalem, we visited this hill, ascending from the Valley of Hinnom up long flights of steps. Among the buildings on the summit of the hill we were shown the Cœnaculum, or supposed Room of the Last Supper. It appears today as a large cool room, with arches and columns, and was probably part of a medieval monastery. Nearby we were shown King David's Tomb. Before this mausoleum draped with green, a large number of oil lamps were burning, and pious Jews with their pigtail-like strands of hair were reciting the scriptures in Hebrew. It is most unlikely that this is the burying-place of David, for the ancient city of his time was on Mount Ophel, to the south-east. The tomb, referred to by the Apostle Peter (Acts **2**. 29), must have disappeared when the Romans destroyed the city.

II

Another possible site of the Upper Room and the Last Supper lies well within the walls of the present city. Although it is hidden away in back streets, we were keen to find it. So one day after visiting the Church of the Holy Sepulchre, we managed to get hold of a guide who led us through the narrow streets and winding alleys to the Syrian Church of St. Mark. The Syrian Christians believe that this is the site of the house of Mary, the mother of John Mark, to which Peter went when he was released from prison (Acts 12. 12). The present Crusader church is built on the site of an earlier one. A kindly priest, in faded, ragged robes, welcomed us in and showed us around, and pointed out a picture of the Virgin and Child which, he said, had been painted by St. Luke! Here everything was old, shabby, archaic. Was this indeed the place of the Last Supper? Did the disciples gather here after the Resurrection? Was this the very place where the fire of Pentecost fell? It must have been somewhere near here, in what was then the Upper City. Beyond that, we cannot know with certainty.

It was during the Supper, wherever it took place, that our Lord girded Himself with a towel and washed the feet of His disciples. On the afternoon of Maundy Thursday, we went to see a modern version of this ceremony at the Armenian Cathedral of St. James, which is in the south-western area of the city. The Patriarch, arrayed in gorgeous robes, washed the feet of twelve Armenian bishops and priests. The excited crowds, the solemn chanting, the constant movement, the candle flames, the clouds of incense, the rainbow-coloured robes, combined to make a rich and splendid spectacle. But it would have been hard to devise anything more out of keeping with the stark simplicity of the original rite!

III

Leaving the Upper Room, the Lord and His eleven disciples (since the traitor Judas had already left, John 13. 30) made their way across the city towards the Garden of Gethsemane. Probably, after leaving the darkened narrow streets, they made use of the great viaduct over the Tyropœon Valley, and entered the Temple Area. As was mentioned in the previous chapter, one broken arch of this bridge, Robinson's Arch, still remains.

" They walk for a time in silence through the dark street, and enter the Temple Court.   There in front of them, glinting in the light of the full moon, was the Golden Vine that trailed over the Temple porch, the type of the life of Israel entwined about the sanctuary of God."   These are the words of Dr. Temple who suggests in his *Readings in St. John's Gospel* that the allegory of the Vine and the Branches was spoken by our Lord, not in the Upper Room, but in full sight of this Golden Vine.

Leaving the temple court by a gate in the eastern wall, Jesus " went forth with His disciples across the Kidron valley, where there was a garden, which He and His disciples entered " (John **18.** 1).   Because there was no room for such places in the crowded city, some of the wealthy citizens had private gardens on the slopes of the Mount of Olives.   Was this garden the property of Mary, mother of John Mark?   Or perhaps it belonged to one of the unknown friends of Jesus, who had given to Him the right of entry at any time, " for Jesus *often* met there with His disciples " (John **18.** 2).   Here Jesus " surrounds Himself with two rings of prayer-supporters, as a king in battle might be surrounded by his body-guard.   At the periphery, near the garden entrance, were the eight; further in, the chosen three were closest to Him," writes R. A. Cole, in the Tyndale Commentary *The Gospel according to St. Mark.*   Jesus withdrew " about a stone's throw ", and being in agony, He prayed, " Abba, Father, all things are possible to Thee; remove this cup from me; yet not what I will, but what thou wilt " (Mark **14.** 36).   Peter the eye-witness, who transmits the story through his companion Mark, records with admirable honesty how he and his two friends failed the Saviour in His hour of need, by falling off to sleep.   When Jesus roused them for the third time, the traitor was already approaching on his terrible errand.

IV

We made many visits to the Garden of Gethsemane, which has been acquired by its present guardians, the Franciscans. In the enclosed garden there are amid the present attractive

6. *"He must needs go through Samaria." The Road to Samaria*

7. *"Our fathers worshipped in this mountain." Mount Gerizim from the Well of Sychar*

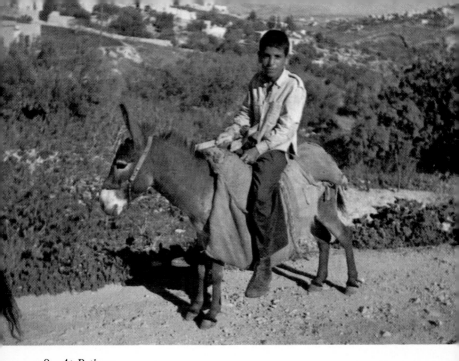

18. *At Bethany*

19. *Pathway from Bethany up the Mount of Olives. In the distance the Mountains of Mo*

. *Jerusalem, showing Siloam, the Kidron Valley and Gethsemane*

. *Temple Area, from the site of the Fortress of Antonia*

22. *Wailing Wall at Jerusalem (remains of Herod's Temple)*

flower beds eight ancient olive trees, the exact age of which is not known. It is not impossible, although it is improbable, that they date back to the time of Christ. As we were staying by Silwan, it was the obvious place to go for a morning Quiet Time. It was good to linger there, with open Bible, talking to God in prayer. Here was beauty and peace—morning sunshine, bright flowers, singing birds. Yet not complete quiet! For along the modern road outside, buses were taking people to work, heavily burdened donkeys were carrying produce into Jerusalem, a shepherd was leading out his flock to pasture. But we realized that there was nothing really incongruous here. For should we not always read the story of Gethsemane, not as something remote and other-worldly, but against the background of the ordinary lives and problems of sinful men?

On this sacred spot Theodosius (A.D. 379–393) erected a basilica (a little bit of the mosaic floor can still be seen), which was destroyed by the Persians and re-built by the Crusaders. Because the present basilica, completed by the Franciscans in 1924, was built by gifts from many lands, it is commonly called the " Church of All Nations ". It has six columns supporting twelve cupolas, and alabaster windows which admit a dim white and purplish light. The effect is one of evening twilight, and is deeply moving. In the middle of the sanctuary is the supposed Rock of the Agony, surrounded by ironwork suggesting sharp thorns. Quite close to this church on the other side of the garden, and just across the narrow road that comes down the western slope of the Mount of Olives, is the Tomb of the Virgin, also called the Church of the Assumption. A descent of forty-five steps is made into what has the appearance of a large crypt; and separated from the surrounding rock is a sizeable tomb, said to be the tomb of Mary. A church has stood on this spot since the fifth century. Outside in the streets, in the course of our several visits to Gethsemane, we had chats with young Arabs about some of their acute national problems. From one, whose home was in Bethany, we bought a shepherd's sling. He was unemployed, he had no money—but he informed us that he was about to be married the next week!

G

V

Judas had given the soldiers a sign by which they might identify Jesus. " ' The one I shall kiss is the man; seize Him and lead Him away safely.' And when he came, he went up to Him at once, and said ' Master! ' And he kissed Him. And they laid hands on Him and seized Him " (Mark **14**. 44–46). After arresting Him, the soldiers, the priests and their followers took Jesus along the Kidron Valley, east and south of Jerusalem, which would have been the shortest and most convenient way to the house of Caiaphas the high priest. Let us reverently follow Him down this King's highway, and describe what can be seen today. The Kidron Valley begins at the foot of Mount Scopus, north of Jerusalem, and passes beneath the eastern wall of the city, which it therefore divides from the Mount of Olives. It has also been called the Valley of Jehoshaphat and has traditionally been regarded by both Jews and Moslems as the scene of the final judgment. For this reason it is a favourite burial place, in part almost covered with tomb-stones. The brook in the bottom of the deep ravine nowadays contains water only after heavy rains. Kidron is mentioned in the Old Testament in connection with the story of David, for at the time of Absalom's rebellion, the king was compelled to cross this valley. " The king crossed the brook Kidron, and . . . went up the ascent of the Mount of Olives, weeping as he went, barefoot and with his head covered " (2 Sam. **15**. 23, 30). In the time of Christ, as was mentioned in the previous chapter, it was spanned by a viaduct.

After passing beneath the eastern battlements, the Kidron Valley bends westwards to the south of the city. Near this bend, at the south-eastern corner of the city walls, in our Lord's time the pinnacle of the Temple towered above the chasm. One views the lofty height today and remembers the fierceness of the Master's temptation, as recorded in Matt. **4**. 5. To the left, travelling southward down the valley, the wall of the city to our right, are four conspicuous tombs or monuments, one of which is associated with Absalom, and another

with the prophet Zechariah.   The former, known as Absalom's
Pillar, may be the tomb of the Maccabean ruler Alexander
Jannæus, who died about 75 B.C.   On the night of His arrest,
the Saviour must have passed close by these monuments.   We
remembered that as our gaze lingered upon them.   We
descended westwards, and could see the Arab village of Silwan
(the Biblical Siloam) over there to the left; to our right Mount
Ophel, the original site of Zion.

VI

When the Hebrews conquered Canaan they were unable to
capture Jerusalem, the stronghold of the Jebusites.   This, the
original city, stood on the spur of Ophel to the south of the
present city wall.   The fortress was so strong that the Jebusites
regarded it as impregnable.   When therefore David advanced
to attack it, they taunted him from the walls: " You will not
come in here, but the blind and lame will ward you off " (2
Sam. 5. 6).   The capture of the city was a brilliant military
exploit, for Joab and his soldiers secretly climbed up the water-
channel and surprised the over-confident defenders from within (2 Sam. 5. 8; 1 Chron. 11. 6).   This may have been the
water-shaft in the solid rock above the Virgin's Spring.   By
this means, without leaving the city, the garrison could draw up
water from the pool beneath.

This problem of an assured water supply during a siege was
solved by a later king in a different way.   In the Bible we read
of " the deeds of Hezekiah, and all his might, and how he made
the pool and the conduit and brought water into the city " (2
Kings 20. 20).   From Gihon or the Virgin's Spring, Hezekiah
cut a tunnel under the mountain, which brought the water inside the city to the Pool of Siloam.   This narrow tunnel, which
is over 1,700 feet long, has two shafts to the surface, and is bent,
probably to avoid obstructions.   In 1881, an inscription in
ancient Hebrew was found on the walls of the tunnel about
nineteen feet from the outlet into the Pool of Siloam.   It tells
how, working from opposite ends, the two groups of workmen
managed to meet in the middle.   One evening after supper, we

made up a party and went down the Kidron Valley by car to the Virgin's Spring. Equipped with lanterns and candles, we descended the 32 steps to the spring, and waded into the cold water. " The waters of Shiloah that flow gently " (Is. **8**. 5), varied in depth, rising in places right up to the thighs.

Slowly, and for some of us painfully (for it was like walking with bare feet on a stony beach), we made our way through the twisting tunnel, mostly able to stand upright, and lustily singing " Onward Christian Soldiers " and other hymns. We were probably rather more cheerful than the soldiers of Hezekiah, threatened by the invasion of Sennacherib the Assyrian. But it is not an exploit to be attempted in your Sunday clothes, and it seems to be a very long third of a mile before you emerge into the Pool of Siloam. It was to this pool, then (but not now) inside the city walls, that Jesus sent the blind man to wash the clay from his eyes, " saying to him, ' Go, wash in the pool of Siloam ' . . . . So he went and washed and came back seeing " (John **9**. 7). The ruins of a church erected here in the fifth century are still visible. We visited the pool at different times of the day. The women of Siloam were washing their clothes in the pool in the mornings, and the local boys were using it as a bathing pool in the evening. Today it looks neglected and unattractive.

VII

As you walk down the Kidron Valley south-westwards past Gihon where Solomon was crowned, it is difficult to realize that in Biblical times the south wall of Jerusalem, now so much further to the north, overlooked this valley. Somewhere here stood the great tower of Siloam, which collapsed suddenly and killed eighteen men. The Saviour made reference to this event, as recorded in Luke **13**. 4. A little south of the Pool of Siloam, the Kidron Valley runs into the Valley of Hinnom, which comes down to it from the west. They meet at what is called Job's well. Here it was that Adonijah, aspiring to succeed David as king, " sacrificed sheep, oxen, and fatlings by the Serpent's Stone, which is beside En-rogel, and he invited all

his brothers, the king's sons, and all the royal officials of Judah "
(1 Kings 1. 9). His party broke up in confusion and panic,
however, when they heard the acclamations which accompanied
the coronation of Solomon at Gihon, further up the valley (1
Kings 1. 39–41). Adonijah was obviously able to hear the
rejoicing, but not near enough to see what had taken place.
Near En-rogel, on the southern slope of the Valley of Hinnom is
Akeldama, the Field of Blood, bought with the thirty pieces
of silver, the price of Judas' betrayal (Acts 1. 18, 19).

It was not possible for us to walk right up the valley of
Hinnom to the foot of the (so-called) Mount Zion, described at
the beginning of this chapter, for part of this is in Jordan and
part in Israel. It was in this deep gorge that the apostate kings
Ahaz and Manasseh offered worship to Molech, making their
children pass through the fire (2 Chron. **28**. 3; and **33**. 6). For
this reason it was defiled by good king Josiah (2 Kings **23**. 10),
and thereafter became the tip-heap, the receptacle of the city's
refuse—a place of flames, worms, corruption and death. It
became, therefore, a symbol of the realm of punishment and
perdition beyond death—" black Gehenna called, the type of
hell," writes Milton in *Paradise Lost*. The Lord Jesus referred
to this when He said, " It is better for you to enter the kingdom
of God with one eye than with two eyes to be thrown into hell
(Gehenna—Ge-hinnom, or Valley of Hinnom), where their
worm does not die, and the fire is not quenched " (Mark **9**.
47, 48).

VIII

We do not know just how far down the Kidron Valley Jesus
was led on the night of His arrest. At some point the procession
of soldiers and priests with the Saviour must have passed
through a gate in the south wall, and begun the steep climb to
the palace of the high priest. The Assumptionist Fathers have
excavated a flight of ancient steps, which lead up from the Pool
of Siloam towards Mount Zion. These slabs of stone in the
hill-side may have been there in our Lord's time, and as this is
the shortest way from Gethsemane to the Upper City, it is at

least possible that the feet of our Redeemer trod these very stones. They lead in the direction of the Church of St. Peter Gallicantu (The Church of the Cock-crow).

The Augustinian Fathers believe that this church of theirs is built on the site of the house of Caiaphas, and that here it was that Peter denied his Master (John **18**. 15–19). We spent some time looking at the buildings and the caves below, said to have been guard-rooms. One pit-like cell is pointed out as the very dungeon in which the Saviour spent some hours that night! Was our Lord tried and imprisoned here? There is very little evidence for this identification, and it is better to admit that it is not really known exactly where the house of Caiaphas stood. It would certainly have been on this side of the Tyropœon Valley, perhaps near here, somewhere in the Upper City of our Lord's time. There He was examined during the night by Annas and Caiaphas, and very early next morning was condemned to death for blasphemy at a formal meeting of the Jewish Sanhedrin. His earthly journey was almost over. His feet were about to tread the last road—the way of sorrows, the way to the Cross.

CHAPTER ELEVEN

THE WAY OF SORROWS

I

THE CHRISTIAN VISITOR to Jerusalem today can never forget that this is the holy city, the great city where our Lord was crucified (Rev. **11**. 8). For this reason there are several sacred sites that he will want to try to identify. For example, where exactly did Jesus stand within these walls at His trial before Pontius Pilate? Where is the street along which He walked and stumbled bearing His cross? Can we identify " the place called Golgotha " where they crucified Him? And where exactly stood the tomb from which He rose triumphant?

Not one of these sites can be identified today with absolute
certainty.   For one thing, over the ancient city there has ac-
cumulated an enormous mound of debris, the growth of many
centuries, and this may vary in depth from thirty to seventy feet.
Many secrets, including the exact course of the city walls in the
time of Christ, still lie buried beneath this enormous accumula-
tion.   The Jerusalem of the Gospels lies buried far beneath the
Jerusalem of today—and only here and there can we look down
into it.   And, of course, we must also put out of our minds any
idea that the buildings, the streets, the city walls and gates seen
today were there in the time of Christ.   The present impressive
walls were built by the Turks, under their great ruler Sultan
Suleiman the Magnificent, about A.D. 1540-42.   In these
walls, which are about two and a half miles in circumference,
there are thirty-four towers and eight gates—the New Gate,
Damascus Gate and Herod's Gate in the north wall; St.
Stephen's Gate and the Golden Gate (walled up by the Turks
in A.D. 1530) in the east wall; the Dung Gate and Zion Gate in
the south wall, and the Jaffa Gate in the west wall.

We must note—and this is very important—that the *northern*
part of the area enclosed within *these* walls, lay *outside* the northern wall of the city in Christ's time.   That is why Golgotha and
the Tomb, which lay just outside the city walls when Christ was
crucified and buried, could now be well within the present city
walls.   In other words, the city of Jerusalem has spread
northwards since Bible times.   On the other hand, the Biblical
Jerusalem extended a good way south of the *present* city walls,
and included the whole area right up to the edge of the valleys
of the Kidron to the south-east and of Ge-Hinnom to the south-
west.

There is also another big difference between the Jerusalem
Christ saw, and the old city we see today.   Not only did it lie
as a whole much further to the south, but it was divided from
north to south by the curved Tyropœon Valley, now extensively
filled up, but still visible.   The area to the east of this depression
was called the Lower City, and was bounded on the north by
the Temple Area and the Fortress of Antonia.   To the west of

*divided Biblical
Jerusalem with todays city*

the Tyropœon Valley—called the Valley of the Cheese-makers
—was the Upper City, where King Herod had built his magnificent palace. We have already mentioned in Chapter Nine
that a viaduct led from the Upper City across this valley into
the Temple courts.

It must again be emphasized that the buildings and walls of
Christ's time have almost entirely disappeared. From the
fragments which have been discovered or excavated, together
with hints from the Jewish historian Josephus, it is still not possible to know with any degree of assurance just exactly how the
walls ran in our Lord's time.   That is one reason why we cannot define with certainty the actual Way of Sorrows, or the site
of Golgotha to which it led.   But we *do* know that it was here
in this city, perhaps quite near or even at the traditional site
that the Saviour " bore our sins in His body on the tree "
(I Peter **2**. 24).

II

Very early, about six o'clock on Good Friday morning, Jesus
having been condemned by the Sanhedrin was bound, led from
the House of Caiaphas, the high priest, to the Prætorium, and
handed over to Pontius Pilate.   " Then they led Jesus from the
house of Caiaphas to the prætorium.   It was early " (John **18**.
28).   The prætorium was the official residence of the Roman
procurator or governor, who was staying in Jerusalem, instead
of his capital Cæsarea (see page 39) to keep order at Passover
time.   It was in the city of Jerusalem—but where exactly?
According to the experts there are two possibilities, the Palace
of Herod the Great and the Fortress of Antonia.

The former was in the Upper City, probably not far from the
House of Caiaphas.   On the site of the palace of the Hasmo-
næans, the Maccabean priest-kings, Herod had built his magnificent palace.   Inside, it was luxuriously decorated and furnished; outside, there were numerous porticoes and irrigated
gardens.   Adjoining it to the north, he erected three enormous
towers, which according to Josephus " were for largeness,
beauty and strength beyond all that were in the habitable earth ".

They were named after his friend Hippicus, his brother Phasæl and his wife Mariamne. The remains of one of these towers can still be seen today at the Citadel of Jerusalem near the Jaffa Gate. This Citadel was built by the Moslem rulers of Egypt in the fourteenth century, making use of the foundations and walls of the castle built by the Crusader kings of Jerusalem in the twelfth century A.D. The big tower by the entrance to the Citadel is called " the Tower of David ". The huge blocks of masonry at the base of this tower, which reminded us of those at the Wailing Wall, date like the latter from the time of Herod the Great. They are in fact the remains of one of the three great towers—probably Phasæl—and were there in the time of Christ. Why were they left standing when the rest of the city was destroyed? Because the Citadel was used as a garrison for their own soldiers when the Romans sacked Jerusalem in A.D. 70.

It is possible that Pontius Pilate was residing in this part of Jerusalem, and that the trial of Christ took place at the palace of Herod the Great. We know that at Cæsarea on the coast, the Roman procurators resided " in Herod's prætorium ", i.e. in the palace built by Herod (Acts **23**. 35). This suggests that when at Jerusalem the procurators might also have resided in Herod's former palace. Furthermore, it is more likely that Pilate's wife, who intervened in the trial, would be living here, rather than in the grim Fortress of Antonia. We remembered her words, " While he (Pilate) was sitting on the judgment seat, his wife sent word to him, ' Have nothing to do with that righteous Man, for I have suffered much over Him today in a dream ' " (Matt. **27**. 19). Also, from this place Pilate could more easily have sent Jesus to Herod Antipas who would be residing in this part of Jerusalem. " And when he learned that He belonged to Herod's jurisdiction, he sent Him over to Herod, who was himself in Jerusalem at that time " (Luke **23**. 7). These points taken together do not amount to proof; they can do no more than suggest, as a possibility, that the palace of Herod the Great was the prætorium, where Jesus Christ stood before the governor.

III

The other possibility, backed by a greater weight of tradition and scholarship, is that the trial of Jesus took place at the Fortress of Antonia.   Unlike the eastern and southern approaches to the city, which were protected by the deep valleys of Kidron and Ge-hinnom, the northern approach to the city was without natural defences.   For this reason, in ancient times, a strong fort was built north of the Temple Area.   In his autobiography, Nehemiah speaks of procuring " timber to make beams for the gates of the fortress of the temple " (Neh. 2. 8).   On this same site the Maccabean rulers built a castle called Baris.   Josephus who supplies this information adds that " when Herod became king, he rebuilt that castle, which was very conveniently situated, in a magnificent manner, and because he was a friend of Antonius (i.e. the Roman, Mark Antony), he called it by the name of Antonia ".

During the time of Christ it was used by the Roman soldiers as a barracks.   " Very conveniently situated," as Josephus says, just north of the Temple, it commanded a view of the sacred courts, and enabled the watchful garrison to keep an eye on the turbulent crowds at Jewish festivals.   This is one important reason why Pilate might have been residing here at Passover time; he would be right on the trouble spot!   The ancient fortress covered quite a large area, and a number of different buildings now stand on the site.   They are divided by the street which runs westwards into the city from the eastern gate of St. Stephen.   We shall begin our journey from this gate, and describe one of several visits we made to this site.

IV

Walking up the Kidron Valley, past the Garden of Gethsemane, we followed the road left to enter the city by the only open gate in the eastern wall.   In Arabic this is called Bab Sitti Marian (St. Mary's Gate), but it is usually known as St. Stephen's Gate, since for long it has been assumed that near this spot the first Christian martyr was stoned (Acts 7. 58).   Another suggested place of Stephen's death is north of the Damascus Gate, along the road to Samaria just beyond the Garden Tomb. There today stands St. Stephen's Convent, the home of the Dominican Fathers. Approaching St. Stephen's Gate we stopped to photograph a beggar squatting in the roadway like Bartimæus outside Jericho (Luke 18. 35). Clicks—*baksheesh*— smiles all round —a few words of greeting, and we were ready to enter the old city.

Just inside the gate we passed to the right into " the Enclosure of Saladin " which contains the Crusader Church of St. Anne and the excavations of the Pool of Bethesda. The church is so called, because Anna and Joachim the parents of the Virgin Mary are said to have lived in the grotto beneath. There is no authentic evidence for this tradition, or for the belief that the Virgin Mary was born here. The church itself is a fine example of Crusader architecture and, in its unspoiled simplicity, is among the most lovely of all the churches in the Holy Land. It was preserved at the time of the Moslem conquest, because the Saracen general Saladin made it into a college for the study of the Koran.

Crossing the compound, we then went to see the excavations, still continuing, of the Pool of Bethesda. In the time of Christ this pool was just outside the northern wall of the city, and was a meeting-place for invalids, since the water, which was disturbed from time to time by a spring, was believed to have healing properties. " Now at the Sheep-Pool in Jerusalem there is a place with five colonnades. Its name in the language of the Jews is Bethesda. In these colonnades there lay a crowd of sick people, blind, lame, and paralysed " (John 5. 2, 3, N.E.B.). Here Jesus healed the man who had been crippled for thirty-eight years. The pool was buried for centuries beneath the debris of the city, but recent excavations have revealed two basins, a double pool, divided in the middle by a wall. The pool is mentioned by a number of early Christian writers, Origen, the Bordeaux Pilgrim (A.D. 333) and Cyril of Jerusalem. There was a church here as far back as the fourth century. Holding on to a flimsy hand-rail, and descending steep

steps below ground, we saw one of the pools.   With what devotion some were lingering there, filling little bottles with the water!

V

After leaving Bethesda, we continued westwards from St.
Stephen's Gate until we reached the Arch of the Ecce Homo
which spans the street.   This certainly is an ancient arch.
When Hadrian rebuilt Jerusalem in A.D. 135, a new city with
the new name Aelia Capitolina, he erected an eastern gate with
three arches.   The centre one of these is that now seen spanning
the street.   Today the buildings on both sides as well as the
street itself are over the site of the ancient Fortress Antonia.

We turned from the roadway to the right, and entered a
courtyard made bright and attractive with flower beds.   In
front was the Franciscan Biblical Institute, to the left the Chapel
of the Condemnation and the Imposition of the Cross, to the
right the Chapel of the Flagellation.   A little further down the
street, also on the right, we entered the Convent of the Sisters
of Zion.   One of the Sisters, acting as guide, gave a short and
very interesting description of the buildings, and then led us
down into the chapel.   Immediately over and behind the altar,
itself built of stones from the Way of Sorrows, was the third
arch of Hadrian's eastern gate.   But we were to descend deeper
into the building before seeing one of the most impressive sites in
all the Holy Land.   Down a flight of steps from this chapel to the
ground level of the city in Christ's time,—we were standing on
the actual pavement of the courtyard of the Fortress of Antonia.

It was probably on this very pavement that the public part of
the trial of our Lord took place.   " When Pilate heard these
words, he brought Jesus out and sat down on the judgment seat
at a place called The Pavement (Greek, *Lithostrotos*), and in
Hebrew, Gabbatha " (John **19**. 13).   The huge stones were
deeply grooved, perhaps to prevent horses from slipping, and
there were gutters to carry away the rain.   Some of the flag-
stones bore marks made by the soldiers for their games.   The
Sister who was our guide drew back a piece of matting and
showed us on one of the stones the outlines of a game called

Basilikos (King)—with circle, sword and crown. She suggested that there could have been a connection between this
game of " King ", and the " game " the soldiers played with
Christ as they mocked Him saying " Hail, King of the Jews "
(Matt. **27**. 27–31). We stood silently gazing at the marks made
by the rough soldiers. Those were crude and cruel days.
Here indeed we were on holy ground, treading literally in the
steps of the Master.

VI

On the other side of the narrow street, the buildings are also
on the site of Antonia, and it may have been in this part of the
fortress that Christ was tried in private by Pontius Pilate.
" Pilate entered the prætorium again and called Jesus " (John
18. 33). Here stands the Moslem college of Al'Omariyeh with
its spacious courtyard. Climbing steps on one side of this
courtyard we had a fine view looking southward of the Temple
Area. It must have been from this vantage point that the
Roman officer intervened when the mob was attempting to
lynch Paul. " He at once took soldiers and centurions, and *ran
down* to them." Paul was arrested and bound with two chains,
" and when he came to the steps (i.e. up from the temple court
into the fortress), he was actually carried by the soldiers because of the violence of the crowd " (Acts **21**. 32, 35).

It is from this courtyard today that processions start along
the Via Dolorosa, for this is the Way of the Cross, from the
Prætorium to Calvary. We had first visited this assembly
point on the morning of Good Friday, when the sun was shining
from a cloudless sky upon the motley crowd packed into the re-
stricted space. There were dark-skinned Arab boys perpetu-
ally grinning, women veiled in black, ancient men in flowing
white robes and red turbans, Jordanian soldiers and police,
Greek and Roman priests, friars, monks and nuns, Europeans
from many nations, Arabs, some in modern and some in oriental
dress—even black-skinned Ethiopians. The scene was a blaze
of colour—a paradise for the photographer. There was the
constant movement of people, and a babel of voices in many

languages. The atmosphere was one of excitement, and even
gaiety—rather like that of a village fair! The " call to prayer "
from the adjacent minaret mingled strangely with the chants of
the Christians, for it was also the Moslem holy day and the fast
of Ramadan. Following a full-sized wooden cross, each
national group of pilgrims moved off in procession, singing a
passiontide hymn, and pausing to pray at the nine supposed
" Stations of the Cross " on the way to the Church of the Holy
Sepulchre. (The last five " Stations " are within the church
itself.)

VII

After the Lord Jesus had been sentenced to death by Pilate
and mocked by the soldiers in the barracks, " He went out,
bearing His own cross " (John 19. 17). Weak, bleeding and
stumbling under the weight of this terrible instrument, His con-
dition was noted by the centurion who " impressed " Simon of
Cyrene to carry it for Him (Mark 15. 21). Is the present-day
Via Dolorosa the actual route they followed to Golgotha? If
the Prætorium was Antonia, and if Golgotha was where the
Church of the Holy Sepulchre now stands (this will be discussed
in the next chapter), then today's Via Dolorosa must corres-
pond with the general direction taken by the procession to
Calvary. Of course we must repeat that the level of the street
in A.D. 30 was far below the present street level, and the
" Stations of the Cross " (that a certain event happened in a
particular place) are creations of the imagination. Nor is the
Via Dolorosa of today one street—it is rather a route which
turns and meanders along several thoroughfares.

But although the streets have changed, are the men in the
streets, the scenes and the actions so very different? One can
still see the water-seller with his cry and jingling can, the potter
turning the wheel with his feet and shaping the clay with his
hands, the burden-bearer with his enormous load (Is. 55. 1;
Jer. 18. 3; Luke 11. 46). Here, too, is the patient donkey
mending its way through the crowds, the food exposed for sale
in the fly-infested bazaar where buyer and seller together strike

a bargain. Through such familiar scenes Christ must have
passed on His way to Calvary. We must never forget that the
road to Golgotha was an ordinary road, trodden by ordinary
people. Along the Way of Sorrows, crowned with thorns, the
great Servant of mankind walked and stumbled bearing in His
own body the ordinary sins of men, right up to the tree (1
Peter 2. 24, margin).

VIII

At some point the procession must have left the streets, and
passed through the gate, on the way to the hill outside the city
wall. Can this place be identified? Just before entering the
Church of the Holy Sepulchre, we turned aside to visit the
Russian Hospice, and inspect " the Russian excavations " which
have excited a good deal of speculation. Here well below present ground level is a large Roman arch, and an extensive
ruined wall built of great blocks of masonry. Could this, as is
claimed, be part of the second city wall—the northern wall of
Jerusalem in the time of Christ? Is the great arch a gateway
in the wall itself? If so, this could be the gate through which
Christ passed out of the city to the mound nearby. It remains
an open question. Some archæologists believe that the Roman
arch may have been the entrance to a Forum built by Hadrian,
and that the great blocks of masonry may be a part of the
basilica erected by Constantine in A.D. 335.

But as we lingered there in the gloom gazing at these ancient
stones we knew that somewhere near here Christ left the city
which had rejected Him, and after passing a little way along
the high road, ascended Golgotha, or Skull-Hill, " the place of
a skull " (Mark 15. 22). The most likely reason for the name
is that the mound or rock was shaped like a human skull. On
the other hand, the name may have been derived from the fact
that executions were frequent there. According to Scripture,
this hill was " outside the gate " (Heb. 13. 12) and " nigh to the
city " (John 19. 20, A.V.). It was so close to the main highway, that passers-by could hurl abuse at the Sufferer on the
Cross (Mark 15. 29). Here it was that on the hill-top, at nine

o'clock in the morning, the Saviour of the world was crucified between two thieves. " Behold, the Lamb of God, Who takes away the sin of the world!" (John **1**. 29). At three o'clock the same day, after a loud shout of triumph, " It is accomplished! " (John **19**. 30, N.E.B.), He " gave up His spirit ". The Way of Sorrows was ended; the Way of Triumph had begun.

CHAPTER TWELVE

THE WAY OF TRIUMPH

I

" Now IN THE place where He was crucified there was a garden, and in the garden a new tomb where no one had ever been laid " (John **19**. 41). Soon after the death of our Lord on Good Friday, Joseph of Arimathea went boldly to Pilate, and asked for His body. Helped by Nicodemus, he took down the body from the cross, bound it in linen cloths and laid it in the new tomb which " was close at hand ". A great stone was then rolled across the entrance to the tomb. This action was witnessed by some of the women disciples, and after resting on the Jewish sabbath (Friday sunset to Saturday sunset), they returned very early on the first day of the week, with the object of anointing His body in the tomb. To their astonishment they discovered that the stone had been rolled away, and heard a young man in a white robe announce, " He has risen, He is not here " (Mark **16**. 1–8). God had vindicated His Son by raising Him from the dead in a transformed spiritual body of glory. The victory of life was accomplished; the way of triumph had begun.

II

The Christians at Jerusalem, who belonged to " the community of the Resurrection ", were hardly likely to forget the actual tomb where this mighty act of God had taken place. They celebrated this event every week on the Lord's Day of

Site of the Last Supper Room

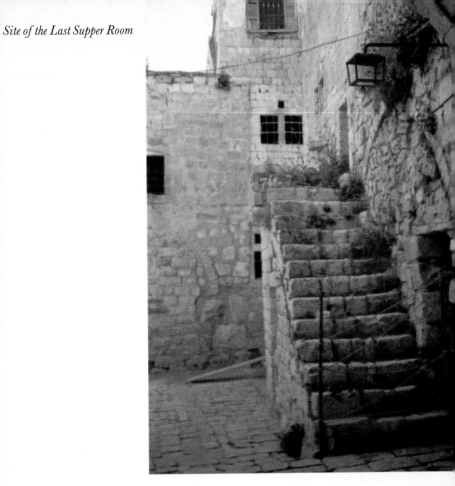

Valley of Hinnom (Gehenna), South of Jerusalem

25. *Ancient Olive Trees in Gethsemane*

26. *"They that had laid hold on Jesus led Him away to Caiaphas." The Way from Gethsemane*

27. (left)
*Ancient steps to the
High Priest's Palace*

28. (right)
Via Dolorosa

29. *Gordon's Calvary*

30. *"He stooping down, and looking in, saw the linen clothes lying." The Garden Tomb*

Resurrection; would they then be likely to forget the actual place? True, their interest was not in the place but in the event. They certainly did not worship " the Holy Sepulchre ", but the Holy Lord, risen and ever-present. But, we repeat, it is quite inconceivable that the Christians at Jerusalem would ever forget the exact location of the " green hill ", which for them was not " far away ", but just outside the city wall. *There* the Saviour had suffered, and " close at hand " had been buried (John **19**. 42).

But it is necessary to enquire whether this knowledge of the exact location of Golgotha and the Tomb possessed by the first generation of Christians survived the destruction of Jerusalem by Titus, at the conclusion of the Jewish war in A.D. 70? Did it survive the Bar Cochba Rebellion of A.D. 132–34, after which Hadrian altered the whole aspect of the city, when he rebuilt it as a Roman colony, with the new name Aelia Capitolina? Was a reliable tradition of the location of these holy places handed down by Christians for 300 years, as a result of which the emperor Constantine was able to erect the first basilica on the spot in A.D. 335? Some say—" Obviously, quite impossible "; others say—" Of course, the Christians would treasure and hand on this knowledge." The fact is that we simply do not know—for sure. According to the Church historian Eusebius, when Hadrian rebuilt the city, he desecrated the holy places by erecting a temple to Aphrodite on the site. This would only serve to mark it more clearly!

The situation was changed, however, when the emperor Constantine professed conversion to Christianity. When his mother Helena arrived in Jerusalem on a pilgrimage in A.D. 326, bishop Macarius told her that Golgotha and the Tomb lay beneath Hadrian's pagan temple. Evidently that was what *he* believed. Helena interested her son Constantine, who ordered the site to be cleared, so that the place of the Resurrection might be made visible. And it was during these excavations, so it was claimed, that the Tomb was discovered, having been covered up but not destroyed by Hadrian. All the hill-side round it was cut away, in order to separate the Tomb and

H

Calvary from the surrounding rock.   There is no doubt whatever that the present Church of the Holy Sepulchre stands over
the area that was cleared and excavated by Constantine.

III

Over the Tomb Constantine built the Rotunda—a large circular building with a dome, called the Anastasis (the Greek
word for Resurrection).   In front of this was a vast court, to
one side of which was the rock of Calvary, which had also been
cut around and isolated.   On the other side of this court from
the Rotunda, he erected a large basilica, with one apse, five
naves and an atrium.   This was known as " the Martyrium "
—the witness.   These magnificent buildings were destroyed by
the Persians in A.D. 614, partly restored by the Abbot Modestus
in A.D. 629, and destroyed yet again by Hakem, Calip of Egypt
in A.D. 1009.   The church was rebuilt by the emperor Constantine Monomachus in A.D. 1048, and it was this building
which was modified and improved by the Crusaders who arrived
in A.D. 1099.   The Crusader church was badly damaged by
fire in A.D. 1808, and the work of rebuilding and repair was
undertaken later under the direction of a Greek architect.   The
present building is the result of his work.

In the course of our journeys through Jerusalem we visited
this church a number of times.   The courtyard in front, beneath which many Crusaders lie buried, is now disfigured by
the great iron stanchions which prop up the building.   The
scaffolding was placed there by the British Government to prevent the structure from collapsing, as a result of an earthquake
in 1927.   Inside the entrance door on the left is the divan of the
Moslem doorkeepers, and immediately in front the Stone of
Unction, which tradition associates with the anointing of
Christ's body before burial.   We observed how some of those
entering, knelt and kissed this stone.   Turning immediately
right, we ascended a stairway to the chapel of Golgotha, or
Calvary (" Calvaria " is the Latin rendering of the Hebrew
word " Golgotha ").   This chapel stands almost fifteen feet
higher than the level of the main church, and is built on the

rock. It is divided; the right half belongs to the Roman Catholics, and the left to the Greek Orthodox Church. The latter, hung with many lamps, adorned with paintings and—to our way of thinking—hideous ikons, gleaming with silver, gold and jewels, was pervaded with the smell of oil and burning candles.

Beneath the altar is a small hole. A bearded priest standing by handed us a taper, and by its aid we could peer down and see the naked rock. Here, they say, the cross of Christ actually stood. They point to a rent in the rock at the side, made by the earthquake (Matt. **27**. 51). There is an old legend that the blood of Christ flowed down through this cleft and touched the skull of Adam who was buried in the grotto beneath. We descended from " the hill " and entered this small dark chapel of Adam, noticing the rent in the bare rock from beneath, and then continued along the ambulatory and down a long flight of steps to the former crypt of Constantine's basilica. Decorated with paintings, this church of St. Helena belongs to the Armenian Community. In the right-hand corner, a further flight of steps leads down to a grotto—the Latin chapel of the " Invention (Finding) of the Cross ". According to another legend, in this cistern at the foot of the hill of Calvary, Helena mother of Constantine, found the cross of Christ and the crosses of the two thieves. Three hundred years after the event!

Returning from these chapels along the ambulatory on the other side of the Catholicon (the main, central, Greek Orthodox " choir " of the Church, now shored up with massive beams), we came to the Rotunda—the large, circular, domed building over the supposed site of the Holy Sepulchre. Here right in the middle there is a huge, ornate and ugly structure, erected in the nineteenth century over the Tomb. We waited our turn to enter; then found ourselves in a small chapel called the Chapel of the Angel. A fragment of the great stone on which the angel sat is included, so it is claimed, in the pedestal right in the centre. To the left and right are tiny openings, through which the " holy fire " is passed on Easter Eve. A very low door leads into the Tomb, which is covered over by a large slab of marble.

We bent down, went through, and looked around.   Inside this tiny place, which only two or three people may enter at a time, stood a bearded monk in his black cassock.   Beside him there was an offertory plate!

IV

We found the Church of the Holy Sepulchre depressing and even repellent.   The structure itself is in a deplorable state of dilapidation and neglect.   Did the nineteenth century Greek architect have a plan, or a nightmare?   What an unrelated jumble of chapels and dark meandering passages!   Have eastern Christians no æsthetic sense, that they should adorn their chapels with cheap tinsel, garish ikons and hideous pictures?   How incongruous to adorn Mount Calvary with gold, silver and costly jewels!   Where amid all these complicated rites, mournfully chanted in archaic language, is to be found " the simplicity which is in Christ " (2 Cor. **11**. 3, A.V.)?   There were times when exploring dark passages alone, right away from groups of tourists or pilgrims, we were almost frightened as suddenly out of the gloom a column of chanting priests appeared and bore down upon us.   This church of dark shrines, occupied by Greeks and Latins, by Armenians and Copts, is a grim monument of Christian sectarianism and disunity.   Here, where Christ died to make us all one (Eph. **1**. 10), we advertise our division to the world.

Most tragic of all is that the Church of the Resurrection has about it the atmosphere of death.   For the medieval obsession with the physical sufferings and death of Christ, to the exclusion of the life and glory and power of His resurrection, is seen here at its worst.   We cannot do better than repeat Michelangelo's indignant protest: " Why do you keep filling gallery after gallery with endless pictures of the one over-reiterated theme, of Christ in weakness, Christ upon the Cross, Christ dying, most of all Christ hanging dead?   Why do you concentrate upon that passing episode, as if that were the last word and the final scene, as if the curtain dropped upon that horror of disaster and defect?   At worst all that lasted for only a few hours.   But to the end of unending eternity *Christ is alive, Christ rules and reigns and triumphs.*" The Martyrium, the Anastasis—oh, for a true witness to the Resurrection!

V

Happily there are other places, all very near to Jerusalem, where it is much easier to realize the truth of the angelic message " He has Risen ". There is the Garden Tomb, the Way to Emmaus, the Mount of Olives—and to these we now turn. Just to the north of the Damascus Gate, there is a quiet and lovely place known as the Garden Tomb, which we visited on a number of occasions. The enclosed garden is well cared for, and we retain lovely memories of colour and perfume, of peace and quiet, of beauty and life. The good brother in charge quotes freely from the Scripture as he guides tourists round, and never fails to press home the Good News of Christ and His salvation.

The tomb, quarried out of the hill-side, was discovered in 1867. Stepping inside, we found a fairly large ante-chamber, leading into the tomb itself, with its rock shelves on which the dead lay. It was widely held in the nineteenth century, especially among Protestants and evangelicals, that this was the authentic tomb of Christ. Reaction against the garish shrines in the Church of the Holy Sepulchre, and the fact that this tomb was obviously outside the city walls, combined with the simplicity and beauty of the place, strengthened this conviction— for which, however, there is no absolutely convincing evidence. But the tomb of Christ could have been very much *like* this. The Garden Tomb, in a setting simple and beautiful, helps the pilgrim to recapture the scene and atmosphere of that glorious morning on which Christ rose triumphant. Close by is a wine- press, and a very short walk through the garden brings the visitor in sight of Gordon's Calvary—so called because the famous General Gordon believed that this rock-faced hill was the authentic Golgotha. The rock with its deep eye sockets does indeed bear some resemblance to a human skull. Today, it looks down on a bus station, and faces—at a little distance— the present northern wall of Jerusalem. On the top of the hill

itself, which we walked over one evening, there is now a
Moslem cemetery.

The Garden Tomb had helped us to visualize the tomb of
Christ; another place a little further north helped us to realize
what the great stone was like, the stone which blocked the
entrance of that tomb, until the angel rolled it away.   Near to
St. George's Anglican Cathedral, where we worshipped on a
number of occasions, there are the excavated Tombs of the
Kings.   This necropolis belonged to the family of Helen,
Queen of Adiabene, a convert to Judaism, who came to
Jerusalem in A.D. 44.   At a distance of some 500 metres north
of the city, she built this sepulchral monument, in which her
remains and those of her son, Isates, and other descendants
were laid.   At the entrance to these extensive underground
tombs there is a large rolling stone, shaped like a cart-wheel,
about four feet high, and set in a groove.   With our combined
strength, we tried in vain to move it.   Small wonder the women
on Easter morn were asking, " Who will roll away the stone for
us from the door of the tomb?" (Mark **16**. 3).

VI

On that first glorious Easter Day, the Risen Lord appeared
not only to the women at the Tomb, but also to Cleopas and his
friend as they walked to the village called Emmaus.   Over-
taking them as they conversed together they did not recognize
Him; but as He opened to them the Scriptures, showing how
the Messiah must enter into His glory through suffering, their
hearts burned within them (Luke **24**. 13–35).   Where was this
village called Emmaus?   Jerome and Eusebius identify it with
a town twenty miles west of Jerusalem on the Maritime Plain,
called Nicopolis or Emwas.   But Luke says that it was sixty
furlongs (about seven miles) from Jerusalem.   It could therefore be the town of Abu Ghosh, where in commemoration of the
event, the Crusaders built a beautiful church.   We had passed
through this place on our way up the valley from Lydda to
Jerusalem; it is the Kiriath-jearim of the Old Testament,
where the Ark of God remained for twenty years (1 Sam. **7**. 2).

To the north-east of Abu Ghosh, just inside Jordan territory, is the little village of Kubeibeh or Imwas, which again *may* have been the Emmaus of the Gospel. From the old city of Jerusalem it was a pleasant drive to the north-west, over winding paths and stony hills; for unlike Cleopas and his companion we did not walk, except down the final stretch of the road into the village. Recent excavations have shown that there was a village here in our Lord's time. Alongside the ruins of an ancient Byzantine church, there is now a modern Franciscan church built as recently as 1902. The fine sequence of stained glass windows depicts the matchless story—the two men setting out; Jesus interpreting the Scriptures to them; the pressing invitation at the door of the house; the moment of recognition in the Breaking of Bread; Cleopas reporting to the Twelve; and the appearance of the Risen Lord in their midst. On the wall we discovered a plaque with these beautiful words:

> *Easter, morning has come; Easter, care has gone home;*
> *Easter, the Lord is with us; Easter, our hearts do burn;*
> *Easter, our grief has gone. Jesus, Jesus is with us,*
> *To celebrate the feast of love.*

VII

Both within and around Jerusalem, and in their familiar haunts in Galilee, Jesus " showed Himself to these men after His death, and gave ample proof that He was alive; over a period of forty days He appeared to them and taught them about the kingdom of God " (Acts **1**. 3, N.E.B.). On that fortieth day, He appeared for the last time. He led them out over against, or as far as, Bethany, " and lifting up His hands He blessed them. While He blessed them, He parted from them and was carried up into heaven " (Luke **24**. 50, 51). The Apostles would certainly never forget that spot on the Mount of Olives where they last saw their beloved and glorified Lord. The tradition would be preserved by the local church. In A.D. 378 a Roman lady named Pomenia erected a polygonal building on the supposed site. That has long since disappeared;

and in its place there is now a central edicule or shrine surrounded by an octagonal court. Inside the edicule is the bare
rock—said to bear the imprint of our Lord's footstep! It
adjoins a mosque. Both Christians and Moslems (who believe
in the Ascension) worship on this spot.

* * * * *

We had been toiling up the slope of the Mount of Olives, and
were glad to rest in the sun on the flat roof of the outer court.
What a marvellous view there is from the summit of this mountain! To the west we were looking over the city of Jerusalem
spread out below; to the east we could see the desolate wilderness reaching to the Dead Sea and the mountains of Moab.
But it was neither west nor east that the Apostles were looking
on that Ascension Day. They stood here gazing *up* into
heaven. And the early Church continued to do this, not literally but spiritually. They were not looking back wistfully,
cherishing the memory of a dead Christ. They were looking
up in adoration and trustful obedience to the Risen, Ascended,
Enthroned, Triumphant Lord, Who in due time would return
in glory to complete His Kingdom. They knew that by His
life and ministry, His passion and death, His resurrection and
ascension, He had opened up the way into the presence of God,
into heaven itself.

"Alive for evermore " (Rev. **1.** 18), He still says to us, " I am
the way, and the truth, and the life; no one comes to the Father,
but by Me " (John **14.** 6). Christ Himself is the Way. Today
while some are privileged to visit the Holy Land, the vast
majority of us may not be able to walk literally in the Master's
steps along the highways of Palestine. But we can all walk
the true and living way that our Great Pioneer has opened up
for us. The way to the King is wide open.

GENERAL INDEX

INDEX OF SCRIPTURE REFERENCES